A Guide to... Rosellas and their Mutations

Revised Edition

By Russell Pringle

Edited and Published by ABK Publications © 2009

ABK Publications
PO Box 6288,
South Tweed Heads,
NSW 2486 Australia.

Hard cover ISBN 978 0 9804924 2 2

Soft cover ISBN 978 0 9804924 3 9

COVER PHOTOGRAPHS

FRONT COVER

Top Left
Yellow Rosella by PETER ODEKERKEN

Middle Left
Eastern Rosella by PETER ODEKERKEN

Middle
Blue-cheeked Rosella © Photograph by CYRIL LAUBSCHER

Bottom Left
Green Rosella by MARCUS POLLARD

Top Right
Northern Rosella © Photograph by CYRIL LAUBSCHER

Middle Right
Western Rosella by PETER ODEKERKEN

Bottom Right
Adelaide Rosella by PETER ODEKERKEN

BACK COVER

Crimson Rosella © Photograph by CYRIL LAUBSCHER

Design, Type and Art: edesign

DEDICATION

This book is dedicated to my lovely wife Debbie, for without her efforts, not only would this publication have never eventuated, but I would never have been able to gain the knowledge and experience of breeding the various rosella species that I have over the past 20 years.

CONTENTS

FOREWORD 14
ABOUT THE AUTHOR 15
CONTRIBUTING AUTHOR 15
AVIAN GENETIC CONSULTANT 16
ACKNOWLEDGEMENTS 16
INTRODUCTION 19
Early Records 19
Distinguishing Features 19
TAXONOMY 19
GENERAL MANAGEMENT 21
Selection 21
Sexing 22
DNA Sexing, Surgical Sexing
Bird Seller's Guarantee 23
Government Regulations 23
Transportation 23
Quarantine 25
Catching Net 25
General Maintenance and Cleaning 25
Hospital Box 26
Feather Chewing 26
Worming 27
Parasites 27
Security 28
HOUSING 29
Suspended Aviaries 29
Conventional Aviaries 29
Aviary Size 29
Substrate 32
Framework 32
Walls 33
Roof 33
Walkway 34
Wire 35
The Fit-out 36
Watering Systems
Perches
Hanging Nests
Feeding Stations
Bathing
The Birdroom
Other Considerations 40
FEEDING 41
Seed Diet 42
Pelleted Diet 43
Sprouting Seed 43
Fruits and Vegetables 45

Seeding Grasses and Native Foods 45
Miscellaneous Food Sources 46
NUTRITIONAL REQUIREMENTS 46
Vitamins and Minerals 46
Vitamin A, Vitamin B1 (Thiamine), Vitamin B2 (Riboflavin), Vitamin B3 (Niacin), Vitamin B5 (Pantothenic Acid), Vitamin B6 (Pyridoxine), Biotin, Vitamin C, Vitamin D3, Vitamin E, Vitamin K, Calcium, Chlorine, Iron, Magnesium, Manganese, Protein, Cystine, Lysine, Beta-carotene
Nutritional Composition of Grains 49
International Dietary Examples 49
Diet One—Supplied by Siegfried and Sabine Wiek, Germany
Diet Two—Supplied by Pascal Tellier, France
Diet Three—Supplied by Melinda Schmitz, southern California, USA
Diet Four—Supplied by Roger Meuris, Belgium
BREEDING 52
Compatibility and Bonding 52
Courtship 53
Breeding Season 53
Nesting Logs and Nestboxes 53
Nest Location
Nest Introduction
Heating
Entrance Hole
Inspection Door
Nestbox Lid
Nestbox Ladder
Nest Materials 58
Hardwood Sawdust
Peatmoss
Wood Shavings
Pine Bark
Eucalypt Mulch
Garden Soil
Natural Decayed Timber
Changing Nest Material 59
Nest Inspection 60
Fledging 60
Fledging of a Wild Rosella
Fostering 61
Leg Rings 62
Leg Ring Sizes
Record Keeping 63
Breeding Record Template
Hybridisation 64
Inbreeding 64
Handrearing 64
GROWTH CHARTS 65
HEALTH AND DISEASES 69
Disclaimer 69
General Information 69
Recognising a Sick Bird 70
Keeping Your Birds Healthy 70

Quarantine Procedures 71
Minimising the Spread of Disease 71
Better Health Through Effective Management 72
Checklist for Factors Predisposing Birds to Disease 73

COMMON DISEASES 74
Infectious Diseases 75
Chlamydiosis (Psittacosis)
Gastrointestinal Infections
Intestinal Parasites
Megabacteria
Respiratory Infections
Psittacine Beak and Feather Disease (PBFD)
External Parasites
Non-infectious Diseases and Other Problems 77
Malnutrition
Trauma
Kidney Disease
Liver Disease
Zinc and Lead Poisoning
Reproductive Disease
First Aid for the Sick Bird 78
Basic First Aid for the Injured Bird 79
Things *Not* To Do 80
Supply of Prescription Medications 80

SPECIES 81

EASTERN ROSELLA ***Platycercus eximius*** 82
Other Names 83

DESCRIPTION 83
Adult 83
Cock, Hen
Juvenile 83
Subspecies and Racial Variations 84
P. e. diemenensis, P. e. elecica

IN THE WILD 85
IN CAPTIVITY 86
Status 86
Housing 86
Breeding 86

PRIMARY COLOUR MUTATIONS 87
Blue 87
'Parblue' 87
Cinnamon 87
Dilute Series 89
Dilute
Edged Dilute
Suffused
Fallow 92
'Golden' 92
Lutino 93
NSL Lutino—Recessive Lutino 94
Partial Lutino 94

Melanistic ('Black') 94
Opaline 96
Pied ('Black-eyed Clear') 97
'Dominant Edged' ('Grey-winged and 'White-winged') 98
'Red-fronted' 100
'Yellow-headed' 100

COMBINATIONS OF MUTATIONS 102

Cinnamon Series 102
Cinnamon 'Parblue'
Cinnamon Dilute
Cinnamon Opaline
Cinnamon 'Dominant Edged'
'Yellow-headed' Cinnamon
Lutino Series 105
Lutino Blue—Albino
Lutino Parblue—Creamino
Lutino Cinnamon—'Lacewing'
Lutino Opaline—'Rubino'
Lutino Pied—Lutino 'Black-eyed Clear'
'Yellow-headed' Lutino
Melanistic Series 109
Cinnamon Melanistic—'Cinnamon Black'
Dilute Melanistic—'Dilute Black'
Lutino Melanistic—'Lutino Black'
Melanistic Opaline—'Black Opaline'
Melanistic 'Black-eyed Clear'—'Black Pied'
Opaline Series 115
Blue Opaline
Dilute Opaline
'Dominant Edged' Opaline ('Grey-winged' Opaline and 'White-winged' Opaline)
'Yellow-headed' Opaline
Other Combinations of Mutations 117
'Edged Dilute' 'Dominant Edged' ('Pastel Grey-winged' and 'Pastel White-winged')

BLUE-CHEEKED AND PALE-HEADED ROSELLAS 118

IN THE WILD 120

IN CAPTIVITY 121

Status 121
Housing 121
Breeding 121

BLUE-CHEEKED ROSELLA
Platycercus adscitus adscitus 122

Other Names 122

DESCRIPTION 122

Adult 122
Cock, Hen
Juvenile 123
Subspecies and Racial Variations
'Blue-backed' Blue-cheeked 123

IN THE WILD 124

PRIMARY COLOUR MUTATIONS 124

PALE-HEADED ROSELLA
Platycercus adscitus palliceps 125
Other Names 125
DESCRIPTION 125
Adult 125
Cock, Hen
Juvenile 126
Subspecies and Racial Variations 126
IN THE WILD 126
PRIMARY COLOUR MUTATIONS 127
Blue 127
Lutino 127
Dilute 128
Cinnamon 128
Opaline 130
Pied 130
'Red Suffusion' 131
NORTHERN ROSELLA ***Platycercus venustus*** 132
Other Names 133
DESCRIPTION 133
Adult 133
Cock, Hen
Juvenile 134
Subspecies and Racial Variations 134
P. v. hilli, P. v. melvillensis
IN THE WILD 135
IN CAPTIVITY 136
Status 136
Housing 136
Breeding 136
PRIMARY COLOUR MUTATIONS 137
Cinnamon 137
Opaline 137
'Red-capped' 137
'Red-fronted' 137
COMBINATIONS OF MUTATIONS 137
WESTERN ROSELLA ***Platycercus icterotis*** 138
Other Names 139
DESCRIPTION 139
Adult 139
Cock, Hen
Juvenile 140
Subspecies and Racial Variations 140
P. s. xanthogenys, Blue-backed Rosella
IN THE WILD 142
IN CAPTIVITY 143
Status 143
Housing 143
Breeding 143

PRIMARY COLOUR MUTATIONS 144
Blue 144
Blue-cheeked 144
Cinnamon 144
Dark Factor 145
'Dilute' 145
Faded ('Pastel' or 'Isabel') 146
Fallow 146
Lutino 147
Lutino (Non Sex-linked) 147
Opaline 147
Pied 147
COMBINATIONS OF MUTATIONS 152
Blue Series 152
Fallow Blue
Faded Blue
Lutino Blue—Albino
Blue Opaline
Cinnamon Series 153
Cinnamon Blue
Cinnamon Fallow—'Yellow'
Cinnamon Opaline
Dark Factor Mutations 155

CRIMSON ROSELLA *Platycercus elegans* 156
Other Names 157
DESCRIPTION 157
Adult 157
Cock, Hen
Juvenile 158
Subspecies and Racial Variations 158
P. e. nigrescens, P. e. melanoptera, Blue-fronted
IN THE WILD 160
IN CAPTIVITY 161
Status 161
Housing 161
Breeding 161
PRIMARY COLOUR MUTATIONS 162
Lutino (Sex-linked) 162
NSL Lutino—Recessive Lutino 162
Partial Lutino ('Platinum') 163
Blue 164
Parblue Series 165
Seagreen
Aqua
Turquoise
Cinnamon 168
Yellow 169
Fallow 171
Dilute 172
Pied 172
'Dominant Edged'
'Dark Factor' 175
Opaline 176

COMBINATIONS OF MUTATIONS 177
Lutino Series 177
Lutino Blue—Albino
Lutino Parblue—Creamino
Lutino Cinnamon—'Lacewing'
Lutino Pied
Partial Lutino (Sex-linked)
Platinum Blue
'Yellow' Series 181
Yellow Blue—White
Yellow Parblue
Cinnamon Series 181
Cinnamon Blue
Cinnamon Parblue
Cinnamon Dilute
Cinnamon Yellow
Cinnamon Fallow
Dilute Series 182
Dilute Blue—'Silver'
Dilute Parblue
Dilute Yellow
Fallow Series 182
Fallow Blue
Fallow Seagreen
Fallow Yellow
Pied Series 190
Blue Pied
Parblue Pied
Cinnamon Pied
Fallow Pied
Dark Factor 192
Dark Factor Blue
'Dark Factor' Pied
'Dark Factor' Cinnamon
'Dilute Yellow Dark Factor'

YELLOW ROSELLA ***Platycercus flaveolus*** 194
Other Names 195
DESCRIPTION 195
Adult 195
Cock, Hen
Juvenile 196
Subspecies and Racial Variations 196
IN THE WILD 196
IN CAPTIVITY 197
Status 197
Housing 197
Breeding 197
PRIMARY COLOUR MUTATIONS 198
Cinnamon 198
'Dilute' 198
Lutino 199
Pied ('Black-eyed Clear') 199
'Dominant Edged'

COMBINATIONS OF MUTATIONS 201
Cinnamon Pied 201

ADELAIDE ROSELLA ***Platycercus adelaidae*** 202
Other Names 203
DESCRIPTION 203
Adult 203
Cock, Hen
Juvenile 203
Subspecies and Racial Variations 204
P. a. subadelaidae, P. a. fleurieuensis
IN THE WILD 205
IN CAPTIVITY 205
Status 205
Housing 205
Breeding 205
PRIMARY COLOUR MUTATIONS 206
Blue 206
Cinnamon 206
Lutino 207
Pied 207
COMBINATIONS OF MUTATIONS 207

GREEN ROSELLA ***Platycercus caledonicus*** 208
Other Names 209
DESCRIPTION 209
Adult 209
Cock, Hen
Juvenile 210
Subspecies and Racial Variations 210
P. c. flindersi, P. c. henriettoe
IN THE WILD 210
IN CAPTIVITY 211
Status 211
Housing 211
Breeding 212
PRIMARY COLOUR MUTATIONS 212
Cinnamon or Dilute 212
Pied 212
Colour Variations 213
COMBINATIONS OF MUTATIONS 213

BIBLIOGRAPHY 214

FOREWORD

Australia—also known as the land of parrots—is a continent of many unique and contrasting environments. As an island that has been isolated for millions of years, it is home to flora and fauna—such as the stunning rosella family of parrots—found nowhere else in the world.

Australians often take these beautiful parrots for granted as they are seen flitting around parks and gardens and frequenting backyards. If these birds were not native to Australia, I am sure that we would be even more excited than usual to be visited by one of these beauties.

The eight rosella species and their subspecies are found in their respective geographical locale throughout the country. Although they may vary in size and colour, all species of rosella are distinct in their display of a scallop pattern on the back, are of similar shape and share similar feeding and nesting habits.

In 1988 ***ABK Publications*** published its first book on this species. In 1990 an upgraded edition—***A Guide to Rosellas and their Mutations*** was published—the first in the acclaimed ***A Guide to...*** series of avicultural books published by ***ABK Publications*** since 1987—now regarded among the best captive bird books available worldwide.

Some 20 years later it was time for a completely revised edition incorporating the latest colour mutations and combinations bred in Australia and internationally as well as the improved knowledge on keeping and breeding these wonderful birds.

Hunter Valley aviculturist Russell Pringle accepted the challenge to write this comprehensive revision. Russell keeps many species of parrots and is recognised as one of the most proficient rosella breeders in Australia. He has bred most rosella species and been involved in the development of many different colours—particularly in the Eastern Rosella. He continues to work on establishing new colours and their combinations—which will keep him busy for many years into the future.

Russell has an excellent knowledge of genetics and the outcomes of the combination of colours. During the preparation of this book he consulted with Dr Terry Martin BVSc—author of ***A Guide to Colour Mutations and Genetics in Parrots***—an invaluable tool in the pursuit of understanding primary and combination mutations. Russell has also conferred with aviculturists located internationally on the genetic details pertaining to various mutation breedings worldwide.

Due to many new developments and improvements to our knowledge on keeping and breeding rosellas, this book carries extensive updated information. Russell has explained all aspects of selecting and purchasing birds, the importance of quarantining new birds, successful breeding and the major improvements to feeding and the dietary requirements of rosellas. The numerous new developments and improvements in aviary designs, building materials, nestbox designs, incubators and handrearing techniques are also outlined in detail.

Health issues such as worming, the occurrence and treatment of diseases and disorders—presented by Dr Bob Doneley BVSc FACVSc (Avian Medicine)—is an entirely new chapter not presented in the earlier edition.

The plethora of information presented in this book will make the general husbandry, keeping and breeding of rosellas and their mutations a most enjoyable experience for aviculturists of any experience. Enjoy your read!

Peter Rankine
Fellow rosella breeder and friend of the author

ABOUT THE AUTHOR

RUSSELL PRINGLE

Born and bred in the Hunter Valley region of New South Wales, Australia, Russell Pringle has kept various bird species for the majority of his life. During his school years, Russell began keeping and breeding show pigeons, exhibiting at a number of agricultural shows throughout the Hunter Valley region—winning countless ribbons for his Champion show pigeons.

Russell and his wife Debbie were introduced to parrots in 1989. He was given a pair of King Parrots by Debbie's mother who kept a few pairs at her home in Muswellbrook.

Since 1992, Russell has specialised in rosellas, breeding all species except the Green Rosella, endemic to Tasmania.

His breeding complex consists of more than 30 aviaries that he maintains with assistance and support from Debbie. Using his sound knowledge of genetics, his focus is now on breeding mutations of the Eastern, Western and Crimson Rosellas as well as Princess Parrot mutations and a few exotic parrot species.

CONTRIBUTING AUTHOR

DR BOB DONELEY BVSc FACVSc (Avian Medicine)

ABK Publications and the author are most appreciative of the contribution of the *Health and Disease* chapter by avian veterinarian Dr Bob Doneley.

Bob graduated from the University of Queensland in 1982 and worked in small animal practices in Bundaberg, Brisbane, Toowoomba and the UK, before opening his own practice in Toowoomba in 1988. He achieved Membership of the Australian College of Veterinary Scientists in 1991 and was awarded his Fellowship in 2003 after a four-year training program that took him to the UK once and the USA twice.

Also in 2003 he was appointed Adjunct Associate Professor in Avian and Exotic Pet Medicine at the University of Queensland Veterinary Teaching Hospital. In 2004 he was awarded the College Prize by the Australian College for outstanding contributions to veterinary science in Australia. He has twice received Outstanding Service and Commitment Awards from the Association of Avian Veterinarians (AAV).

Bob is a member of the Australian Veterinary Association (AVA), the Australian Small Animal Veterinary Association, the Association of Avian Veterinarians Australian Committee (AAVAC), the Association of Reptile and Amphibian Veterinarians and the Association of Exotic Mammal Veterinarians. He is a past president of the AAVAC and the Darling Downs branch of the AVA.

He has published numerous papers in veterinary journals, a veterinary textbook on bird medicine, has written two chapters for another textbook and lectured extensively.

Bob is an editorial consultant for the Australian publication ***Australian BirdKeeper Magazine*** whose readers are familiar with the regular column that he prepares on all aspects of avian health. Bob has also advised and contributed to various ***ABK Publications*** titles over the years.

AVIAN GENETIC CONSULTANT

DR TERRY MARTIN BVSc

ABK Publications and the author greatly appreciate the knowledge and expertise of world renowned avian geneticist Dr Terry Martin. Terry, while appreciative of the extensive knowledge that the author has on colour mutations and genetics, was kindly available for consultation on the colour mutation content of the title.

Terry began keeping birds at 10 years of age when he was given a pair of Zebra Finches. Colour mutations quickly became his primary interest in this, and other species, which led to a solid knowledge of basic genetics at an early age. In 1988 Terry graduated with a degree in Veterinary Science from the University of Queensland.

He dedicated his ongoing study of birds to the area of genetics, pigmentation and colour mutations and is highly respected in his research field internationally. Terry has also presented at avian and veterinary meetings and conferences, contributed articles to various publications including ***Australian BirdKeeper Magazine*** and various ***ABK Publications*** books. He has authored ***A Guide to Colour Mutations and Genetics in Parrots*** and co-authored ***A Guide to Cockatiels and their Mutations*** both published by ***ABK Publications***.

In 1999 Terry initiated the formation of an international avian genetics discussion group. Since that time he has continuously discussed and studied mutations and genetics of all avicultural species with authorities from around the world.

ACKNOWLEDGEMENTS

ABK Publications and the author, Russell Pringle, sincerely appreciate and thank the following people for their various contributions and support in the preparation of this comprehensive and informative title.

Although many people from around the world have assisted the author, there are a number of people whose assistance he wishes to acknowledge in particular—Siegfried and Sabine Wiek, Günter Ballon and Roger Meuris have literally spent hundreds of hours communicating with him via email providing invaluable information and photographs of rosellas in their collections. Despite not having personally met, these individuals are regarded as old friends by the author.

The revision of ***A Guide to Rosellas and their Mutations*** has involved considerable effort on the part of the author—Russell Pringle. It is this dedication and ethic that Russell has exhibited in producing the accurate, up-to-date and informative detail that made it obvious that Russell was the most suitable author for this revision. The fantastic support that Russell's wife, Debbie, and his family have provided is greatly appreciated.

Further to those acknowledged in this section ***ABK Publications*** would like to make special mention of the three main contributing photographers—Peter Odekerken (Australia), Cyril Laubscher (UK) and Herman Zomer (Netherlands).

Wildlife photography is not an easy task and the time, patience and expertise necessary in quality photography is depicted in the beautiful images which adorn these pages. We also thank Herman Zomer for allowing us to reproduce some lovely images from his own title on these species.

We are most grateful and appreciative of the following people who have either provided photographs or allowed birds in their collections to be photographed as well as providing valuable breeding information.

Australia	Laurie Arnold	Des Bartz	Alan Birrell
	Tricia Belcher	Des Boorman	Eddie Booth
	Greg Brandon	Bruce Brown	Duncan Butler
	Mario Carbone	Anthony Catt	Kevin Catt
	Geoff Chapman	John Cooper	Josh Daly
	Trevor Davis	Wayne Dempsey	Gordon Dosser
	Shane Drew	Dave Fitch	James Frendo
	Allen Friis	Col Gunter	Hank Jonker
	Leo Joseph	Peter Lane	Barry Leggett
	Bob McLeod	Jeff Murphy	Ben Pearce
	Marcus Pollard	Mark Porter	Peter Rankine
	David Renshaw	Bill Roberts	Ross Roberts
	Gerry Rutte	Russell Scott	Stan Sindel
	Chris Smith	Alan Storm	Paul Stubbington
	Kevin Thomson (late)	Bruce Watts	
Austria	Christian Andert	Erich Burger	
Belgium	Leo de Bot	Marcel Deprez	Roger Meuris
	Frans Nys	Ben Van Looy	Frans Verstrepen
	Louis Verstrepen	Lucien van Schaebroeck	
Czech Republic	Miroslav Beneš—www.mutace-papousku.com		
	Alena Doležalová—Dona Publishing		
France	François Deneaux	Thierry Duliere	Michael Lefebvre
	David Monroger	Pascal Tellier	
Germany	Emil Antonin	Günter Ballon	Hans Biscoping
	Peter Frenger	Uwe Hanisch	Heiner Kastens
	Gerhard Rübesam	Sabine Wiek	Siegfried Wiek
New Zealand	Roy Nichols		
North America	John Rodrigues	Melinda Schmitz	
Netherlands	Herman Kremer	Pieter van den Hooven	
United Kingdom	Peter Addison	Brian Brae	

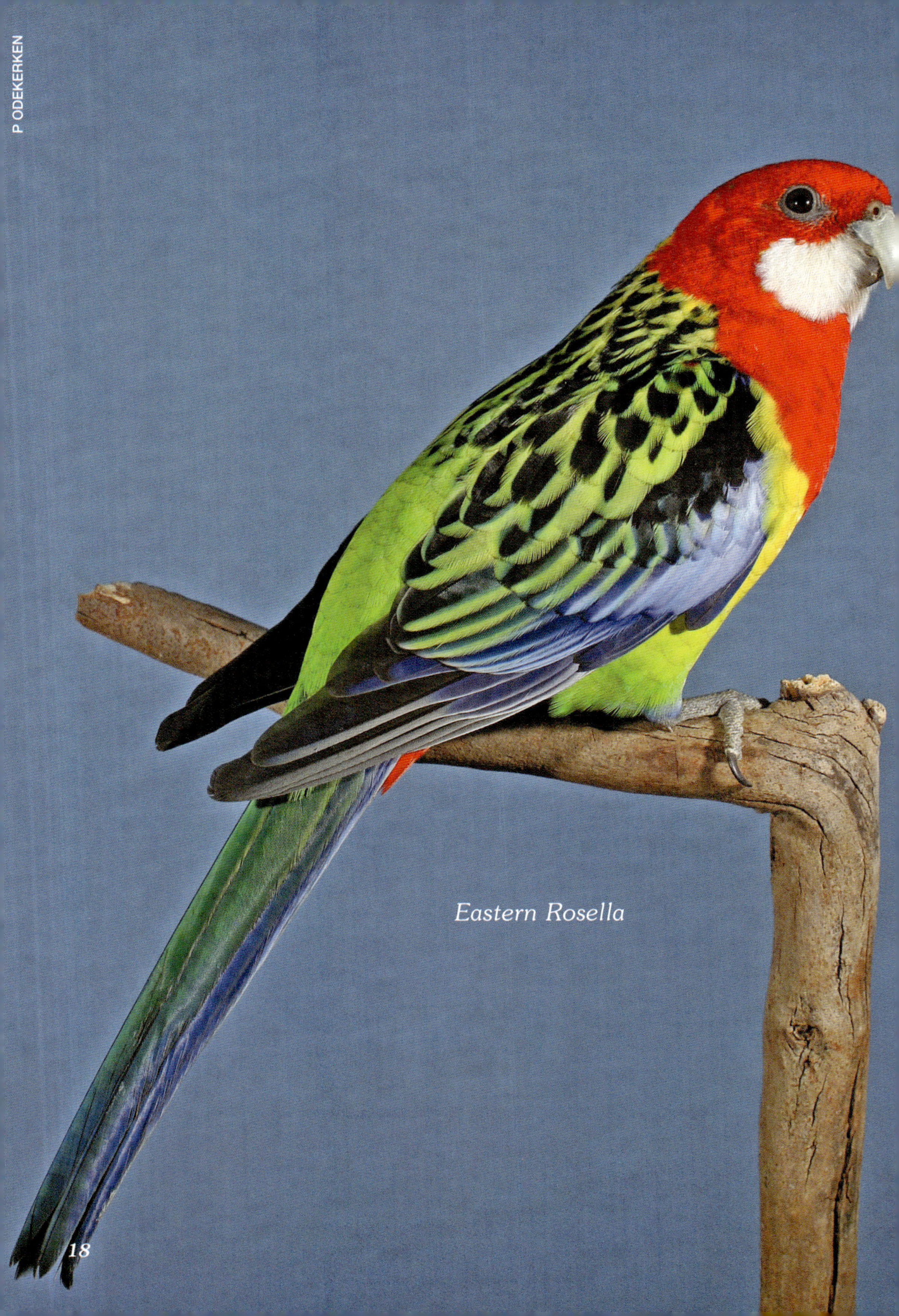

P ODEKERKEN

Eastern Rosella

INTRODUCTION

Crimson Rosella hen

The rosella group of parrots is arguably one of the most recognised of all Australian parrot species worldwide. They are hugely popular aviary subjects in Europe as well as in their native Australia.

The rosella is an ideal parrot for novice aviculturists as they are hardy, quite long-lived and, given the right conditions, will breed readily. Their diet is uncomplicated and they are easily maintained. They are also colourful, reasonably active and usually reasonably priced.

This book has been several years in preparation, the vast majority of this time spent trying to determine the correct naming of the mutations that are held in Australia and, particularly, in Europe.

For the purpose of this book I have endeavoured to identify combinations of mutations by their genetic make-up and, in most cases, avoid the use of 'fancy' names that have been coined by various breeders. Some of the combinations that are held in European collections are known by three or four different names but all are bred from the same primary colours. This was probably the greatest challenge I encountered. And even now, I am still not convinced that all the mutation names published in this book are correct. Those colour names which are questionable have been indicated in inverted commas. While the electronic age has certainly assisted communication worldwide, I did encounter difficulties with translations from other languages and this did take some time to get correct.

Early Records

According to various literature the origin of the name 'rosella' is attributed to the early settlers in Sydney who named the parrot seen around Rosehill, an outer suburb of Sydney, the 'Rosehill Parrot'. This name was shortened to 'rose-hiller' and subsequently shortened again to 'rosella'.

European study of rosellas can be traced back to 1770 when Captain Cook and his party recorded and illustrated the Green, Crimson and Pale-headed Rosellas. The Northern Rosella was first recorded by Robert Brown, a botanist who accompanied Matthew Flinders on his voyage around Australia in the early 1880s—no doubt the reason why this species is commonly known as the Brown's Rosella. The first specimens of the Yellow Rosella were sent to England by Captain Sturt after seeing great numbers of these parrots along the Darling and Lachlan Rivers.

Distinguishing Features

Rosellas are represented in every state and territory of Australia and on some islands in the Bass Strait and off northern Australia. The rosella species are linked by a few distinguishing features—the very prominent cheekpatches, the obvious scalloped pattern on the mantle, the varying shades of blue on the shoulder-patches and the distinctive blue and white edging to the broad tail feathers.

TAXONOMY

Pale-headed Rosella in wild habitat at Buderim, Queensland

The naming and scientific classification of some rosella species and subspecies by ornithologists has been challenging and a complex task that has never had an easy resolve.

For example, the northern form of the Pale-headed Rosella is commonly referred to as the Blue-cheeked Rosella—a similar name to that which some people use to classify the Crimson, Yellow, Green and Adelaide Rosella group of species that display a blue cheekpatch.

In addition, some ornithologists believe that the Yellow and the Adelaide Rosella should be classified as subspecies of the Crimson Rosella.

I will not argue one case against the other but I honestly believe that two species as dissimilar as the Yellow Rosella and the Crimson Rosella are entitled to species status.

For the purposes of this book, I have listed the eight species and relevant subspecies of rosellas that are currently recognised by aviculturists in Australia. As this is primarily a book designed for aviculturists the focus is on such material with an overview of basic taxonomy not deemed to be definitive.

The taxonomic overview of the *Platycercus* genus is as follows:
Order: Psittaciformes
Family: Psittacidae
Subfamily: Psittacinae
Tribe: Platycercini
Genus: Platycercus
Species and Subspecies:
Green Rosella *Platycercus caledonicus*
Crimson Rosella *Platycercus elegans*
Nominate subspecies—*P. e. elegans*
Other subspecies—*P. e. nigrescens* and *P. e. melanoptera*
Adelaide Rosella *Platycercus adelaidae*
Nominate subspecies—*P. a. adelaidae*
Other subspecies—*P. a. subadelaidae*
Yellow Rosella *Platycercus flaveolus*
Eastern Rosella *Platycercus eximius*
Nominate subspecies—*P. e. eximius*
Other subspecies—Golden-mantled Rosella *P. e. elecica* and Tasmanian Eastern Rosella *P. e. diemenensis*
Pale-headed Rosella *Platycercus adscitus*
Nominate subspecies—Blue-cheeked Rosella *P. a. adscitus*
Other subspecies—Pale-headed Rosella *P. a. palliceps*
Northern Rosella *Platycercus venustus*
Nominate subspecies—*P. v. venustus*
Western Rosella *Platycercus icterotis*
Nominate subspecies—*P. i. icterotis*
Other subspecies—*P. i. xanthogenys*

GENERAL MANAGEMENT

Selection

Before purchasing new birds ensure that your aviaries are suitable for housing the rosella species you desire. As unusual as it may seem, unprepared aviculturists have admitted to purchasing birds and transporting them home with no plan of where to accommodate them after quarantine or indeed where to locate the birds during the quarantine period.

Where possible source young, unrelated pairs. True breeding pairs are sometimes available, but this is not common. Most rosellas breed in their first or second year. Be wary of a bird that has not bred—such as a three-year-old hen that has not laid or a mature cock without a mate. The hen may not sit, she may smash her eggs or fail to feed her chicks. A cock may be infertile or attack the hen and the chicks after fledging. Juveniles do not have a breeding history and when they mature should successfully rear young in their first or second year. If the bird is mature enquire as to why the breeder wants to sell it.

It is recommended to purchase birds from an aviculturist. This will allow you to view the parent birds, the aviaries where they are accommodated and their feeding regimen. For example, any variation to the height or the location of the feeding station in your aviaries compared to what the birds are accustomed to requires acclimatisation in a new environment—new introductions must be observed for the first few days to ensure that they have found the feed supply and are indeed feeding.

Be aware of the conditions the birds are kept in—

- Are all birds in the aviary in good condition?
- Are the aviaries overcrowded?
- Are the aviaries clean? If the aviary complex smells of vermin there is clearly a problem—if this is not being addressed, be aware of what else may be neglected.

Look for a bird in good feather, standing erect on the perch and exhibiting clear eyes and nostrils. Observe the bird's physical condition—

- Are the bird's wings in a normal position or are they drooping?
- Is the bird alert or is it sitting in the corner with its eyes half shut? Young rosellas—even when handraised—may be flighty, therefore they should be observed from a distance. Be wary of a juvenile that appears lethargic and remains sitting on the perch or the feed dish when other birds in the cage are active.
- Does the bird fly normally? Short flights around the aviary that leave a bird panting with its mouth open for an extended period may indicate a problem.
- Conduct a thorough physical examination—when you have selected a bird, ask the seller to catch it so you may examine it closely. To assess the body condition and general health, feel the bird's breastbone to ensure it is straight and undamaged and examine the surrounding muscle. A sharp keel bone may indicate health issues.
- Enquire as to when the birds were wormed last. Check there are no faeces stuck to, or staining the vent area.
- Examine the wings and the tail for lice, mites and general condition. Young birds often display broken tail feathers from fighting or from learning to fly in holding cages. This is rarely a problem—be cautious if the entire tail is missing. I prefer to leave damaged or broken tail feathers intact to allow them to moult out naturally, rather than pull them out. Ask the breeder plenty of questions regarding the birds they are offering for sale, including—
  - How old are the birds?
  - Are they related?
  - How does the breeder know they are a pair?
  - Have they been sexed?
  - Are the parents of the birds able to be viewed?
  - If the birds are mature—why is the breeder selling them?

Repeat the same questions in various ways and be wary if you receive inconsistent answers. If you have any concerns at all during the selection, do not proceed with the purchase. It is preferable to wait to purchase good quality birds than to act in haste and later regret the decision.

Sexing

Sexing a rosella can be relatively simple, but it is possible to make the wrong selection. I find it easiest to sex chicks in the nest at approximately three weeks of age before fledging. At this age, cocks are a slightly brighter colour and usually display a short, wide beak. Hens are duller in colour and the beak is narrower.

Over emphasis should not be placed on underwing stripes when sexing—some mature breeding cocks can display traces of juvenile stripes—suggesting the characteristic white underwing is not a reliable indicator of sex. The white underwing stripe is generally absent in the cock *and* hen of the Green, Crimson, Yellow and Adelaide Rosellas and absent in the cock of the Pale-headed, Blue-cheeked, Eastern, Northern and Western Rosellas.

This pair of Pale-headed Rosellas are monomorphic—both the cock and the hen look alike

If you doubt the sex of a bird ask the seller to organise surgical or DNA sexing. A buyer once questioned me about the sex of rosellas he was considering purchasing at a bird sale. I was certain the birds were a pair and I offered to get them sexed by a veterinarian at the sale venue—agreeing that if I was correct, he would pay for the procedure and if I was wrong, I would pay. He was satisfied by my offer and purchased the birds.

There are two primary methods of sexing birds.

DNA Sexing

DNA sexing involves the testing of blood or feathers to identify DNA. It is extremely popular and is a simpler procedure for the aviculturist and less stressful for the bird than surgical sexing—the birds do not have to be transported.

Young birds can be sexed while in the nest or aviary birds caught—a feather sample or a

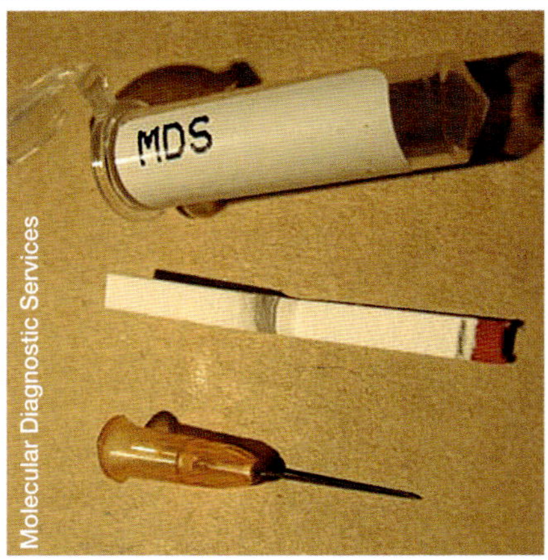

DNA collection kit. Simply prick the bird's toe and touch the end of the paper against the blood spot and place in the tube

pin-prick of blood is taken from the toe and sent to a testing laboratory. Results are sent via fax or email approximately two weeks later.

Surgical Sexing

The surgical sexing procedure has been practised for many years and is relatively safe and accurate. It requires the use of anaesthetic and is performed by a veterinarian.

The advantages of this sexing method are that results are immediate and, at the time of the procedure, the veterinarian can examine the bird's internal organs and general condition.

The main disadvantage is that birds must be transported to and from the aviary and the veterinarian—possibly a day-long affair.

Bird Seller's Guarantee

Aviculturists should provide some guarantee for the birds they sell—under certain circumstances. If a cock is accidentally sold as a hen, the bird should be exchanged or monies refunded—similarly, if a specimen dies from worms or disease within days after the purchase.

Guarantees should not apply if a bird dies of a head injury or from other misadventure or if it dies four weeks or more after being purchased.

In all cases, the onus is on the purchaser to organise a veterinarian to examine the bird or conduct an autopsy if a bird becomes ill or dies.

The late Syd Smith of Victoria—known for his dry sense of humour—gave me some sage advice on how to handle buyers trying to scam the guarantee. He suggested that if a buyer communicated to report the death of a new bird, the seller should tell the buyer to cut the bird's leg off and send the ring back for a replacement bird or a refund. According to Syd, this stopped the non-genuine complaints. While I have never employed this method, I will never forget it!

Government Regulations

Australian aviculturists should consult their state government for details of relevant laws and regulations governing the trading and keeping of native species, such as rosellas. Some states require accurate records to be kept on all rosella species and log books to be surrendered to a specific government department annually. Other states maintain rosellas as species exempt from record keeping.

It is illegal to import foreign or export native birds to or from Australia. However, it is hoped this will change in the future and that Australian aviculturists will have the same opportunities to export and import captive-bred parrots as overseas aviculturists have been doing for many years.

Transportation

Before selecting any birds, ensure you are equipped with suitable carry boxes for the species you intend to purchase. Rosellas can be extremely aggressive, therefore it is vital to transport one rosella per carry box of sturdy construction—do not attempt to transport rosellas in cardboard boxes or small, thin wired cages.

Carry boxes do not have to be expensive—good options are available from most bird shops, through avicultural clubs and societies or at bird sales.

Suitable carry boxes measure approximately 350mm long x 180mm wide x 160mm high or—if a slightly larger size is desired—400mm long x 230mm wide x 230mm high. I recommend a carry box with a door at each end—modify one door by nailing or stapling a piece of thin rubber—with slots cut in it—to the inside. This will prevent the bird escaping back through the hole when released into the box. Leave the other door intact so that it can be opened when releasing the bird—allowing it to simply fly out.

Transportation of rosellas by air or road freight requires the use of a freight box.

These are generally smaller and lighter than carry boxes, due to transit costs being calculated on cubic dimensions and weight. A freight box measuring approximately 290mm long x 120mm wide x 120mm high is suitable for one rosella. A double freight box measuring approximately 425mm long x 250mm wide x 150mm high incorporating two compartments with separate access doors is suitable for transporting pairs of the larger rosella species.

Top, left and right:
Carry boxes designed for transporting one bird per compartment

Freight boxes must be of sturdy construction

Quarantine

Quarantine involves housing a new bird separately from existing birds in a collection—to prevent disease from entering the breeding complex. The quarantine period should be for a minimum of 6–8 weeks. The type of quarantine facility may range from a dedicated quarantine aviary to a small cage kept in a quiet location.

Introduce new birds into quarantine as early in the day as possible. If you arrive home with a bird late in the day, leave it in the carry box until the next morning or place the bird in a small cage and leave a light on so that it may locate food and water during the night. Placing a bird into an aviary near nightfall will cause further stress and it is likely to have difficulty finding food, water and a suitable place to perch for the night.

Birds in quarantine must always be attended to last in the general management and feeding regimen. In order to prevent disease transmission, hands should be washed thoroughly after attending to any bird in quarantine and the bird's food and water bowls should be disinfected separately.

During this period, the droppings should be examined frequently for any irregularities alerting to possible health problems. It is highly recommended to worm birds in quarantine twice and send a sample of droppings to a veterinarian for inexpensive tests to examine the general health and analysis for diseases such as worms, Megabacteria and Psittacosis. Blood samples can also be tested to determine the presence of Psittacine Beak and Feather Disease (PBFD), Polyomavirus and a variety of other health issues. Treat for mites and lice—there are a number of suitable insecticides available.

Any problems experienced during the quarantine period should be communicated to the seller as soon as possible. Most aviculturists will attempt to assist somehow during these early stages.

Once the quarantine period is complete, the bird can be released into a new aviary—only if it is healthy. This should occur in the morning—observe the bird regularly during the first day to ensure it has settled and located food and water. Observation should continue twice a day over the following 7–14 days to ensure the bird has settled into the new environment.

For more information on *Quarantine* see page 71.

Catching Net

A strong catching net is an essential aviary item even if you only have a couple of birds. Suitable nets can be purchased from bird shops or at bird sale vendors. I prefer a dark coloured net as birds tend to shy away from light or bright coloured nets—making catching difficult and more stressful for the birds.

Consider storing a separate net in each aviary bank for quick access. The time saved may mean the difference between life, death or severe injury for a bird.

A strong net is essential for catching rosellas

General Maintenance and Cleaning

It is essential for all responsible aviculturists to develop an efficient and regular aviary cleaning and maintenance program to ensure the continued good health of their birds. A routine will prevent jobs from becoming too big to handle effectively.

Food and water bowls should be removed and cleaned daily and perches changed regularly. Although most nestboxes last for a number of breeding years, it is recommended to replace them every couple of years.

Waste should be removed and the aviary hosed and swept regularly. At least every 1–2 years the aviary should be thoroughly disinfected—use general household bleach diluted at 200mls per 4 litres of water or a commercial disinfectant—then hose the aviaries thoroughly with water. A high pressure cleaner is a more efficient and effective method of cleaning aviaries compared to using a standard garden hose.

Hospital Box

All aviculturists should have a hospital box available for housing any sick or injured birds. The size of this box must be relevant to the species kept—a box measuring approximately 600mm long x 300mm square is suitable for rosellas.

The hospital box should include a heat source—a small heating element, heat pad or light globes—separated from the area where the ill bird is located—and a small fan to circulate the air.

Ensure the hospital box is located in a quiet and warm location and that the bird has adequate food and water.

A heat lamp can be positioned on the top or clipped to the side of a cage using a hospital set-up. Note the distance between the bulb and the cage

Feather Chewing

Feather chewing can be a problem, particularly in the Crimson Rosella. The cause of this behaviour is not clearly understood however, many veterinarians and bird behaviourists suspect it is caused by stress and boredom—a lack of enrichment. It has also been observed in other parrot species.

Feather chewing has been observed in a variety of scenarios and it is more prevalent in cocks than hens. A rosella cock may commence chewing his feathers at the onset of the breeding season and continue while the hen is sitting on eggs—generally stopping this behaviour when the chicks have hatched. His feathers usually grow back following a moult and will remain healthy until the onset of the next breeding season.

I have also observed a rosella cock chew his feathers so aggressively that he struggled to fly. Some cocks have

Rosellas need enrichment in a captive situation—provide branches to chew and climb on

chewed all of their feathers—after being housed with the same mate in the same aviary for a number of years—for no apparent reason.

Some birds also chew the feathers of their mates—this occurs in both sexes. Some hens chew the feathers of their chicks—theories include that this may be an attempt to encourage the chicks to leave the nest so they may lay again, an effort to keep the chicks cool during high temperatures or an act of boredom.

The cause of feather chewing is a complicated health issue

A chick's damaged feathers will usually regenerate after they leave the nest, but sometimes—if the feather follicle has been damaged—the feathers will not re-grow. In this case, the bird will display down in areas where the feathers would normally have grown—this is referred to as the 'fluffy effect'.

Some aviculturists believe feather chewing is hereditary in hens that were chewed themselves—but this is not always the case. However, a hen that chews the feathers of her chicks will usually continue this behaviour in future nests. I have observed a hen that continued to chew chick feathers even after the chicks fledged. This hen had to be removed from the aviary—the cock left to rear the chicks.

Aviculturists have attempted for many years to develop various methods to identify and eliminate feather chewing—with varying results. Although it is not usually a medical condition, it should not be discounted without examination by a veterinarian and medical tests.

The most successful approach to discourage rosellas from feather chewing is to offer branches for the birds to chew and climb on to occupy them. Rope hung in the aviary may also reduce boredom. Ensure any items are non-toxic.

Worming

A regular worming program is vital to the health of captive rosellas. The frequency of worming will depend upon the bird's age and how it is housed.

Young rosellas should be wormed when they are removed from their parents, prior to sale and in autumn. Birds housed in suspended cages or in aviaries with concrete floors will only require worming once a year—generally in autumn.

It is recommended to administer worming medication via a crop needle—the only reliable method of ensuring the correct dosage is administered. A 14-gauge crop needle is suitable for the Western Rosella and a 12-gauge crop needle for all other rosella species.

There are a variety of worming products commercially available in Australia. Aviculturists should consult an avian veterinarian on their use or follow the manufacturer's instructions.

For more information refer to *Health and Diseases* on page 69.

Parasites

Mites are a parasite that sucks the blood of chicks and adult birds. If left untreated they can be lethal. In Australia it is common to find these pests in nestboxes during the breeding season. Therefore, it is essential to inspect the nest regularly. In bad infestations they will crawl up your hands and arms as soon as you attempt to touch the chicks.

The best method of dealing with mites is to spray a safe residual insecticide that—when prepared to the manufacturer's directions—can be sprayed directly onto the birds. The nest will also require a good soaking of insecticide and the nest material replaced.

Bot flies are another problem aviculturists may experience during the breeding season. There are more than 150 species of bot flies around the world—one species can even live in humans.

The Horse Bot Fly *Gasterophilus intestinalis* is the main species encountered in Australia. This bot fly lays eggs in the nest and the larvae—which resemble maggots—burrow into the skin of the chick, where they remain until their life cycle starts again. These pests may be found in the ears, anus and nostrils of captive-bred and wild parrot chicks and also between the toes and in the wings of these birds.

The larvae may be removed with tweezers—this will not harm the chicks and the wound heals quickly—however, do take care during this process.

See *External Parasites* on page 76.

Security

There are a variety of security systems available—trained security dogs, sophisticated electronic alarms and infra-red cameras with laser beams. As a rule, it pays to be suspicious of anyone you do not know when it comes to allowing people access to your home and aviaries.

When planning a holiday, do not broadcast your plans. An effective low-cost security measure is to ensure that a person is always present at your property. This may be difficult, however a house-sitter is highly recommended for long absences. If you are absent, trained dogs—such as Australian cattle dogs—may deter unwanted visitors.

Strangers should not be allowed to inspect your collection. I recommend locating holding cages near the front of your collection—limiting which birds visitors have access to. The maintenance of a log book detailing the names, addresses and license plate numbers of visitors may be a valuable tool if a bird is stolen.

Security cameras can also be used to prevent thefts

In this internet age, avian security has become even more important to prevent the theft of collections by unscrupulous individuals. Be wary of who you do business with over the internet—never disclose your physical address to people you have never met or spoken to. I have had many prospective buyers email me asking for my address—after asking them to phone me I have never heard from them again.

Guard dogs are always a deterrent to potential thieves

HOUSING

When building an aviary for your rosellas remember that what you construct will constitute their entire world. Considerable thought must be put into the design—rosellas are extremely hardy, however they need to be protected from inclement weather. They are also very aggressive—making it necessary to incorporate protection for neighbouring birds.

During the planning stages visit as many aviculturists' complexes as possible and incorporate their best ideas into your own design. Other aviaries often feature innovative details that you may adopt to make management more effective, the birds safer and the environment more enjoyable.

Conventional ground-based aviaries and suspended cages are suitable for housing rosellas—consider space, price and personal preference in your decision.

Although rosellas generally adapt well to a variety of climates, aviaries in all environments require protection from the elements. Australian aviaries should face north or north-east and their southern and western sides should be completely covered to protect the birds from cold winds. Birds housed in south or west facing aviaries will eventually encounter problems. Aviaries must provide birds with access to, and shelter from, the sun and rain.

Suspended Aviaries

Although captive rosellas will reside happily in suspended cages, I am not convinced they are the preferred choice when compared to ground-based aviaries—as rosellas in wild habitat forage on the ground. The advantages of suspended cages are that they are less expensive to build, use fewer construction materials, can be as simple or elaborate as desired and take up less space than conventional aviaries.

Suspended cages or aviaries housing the Western, Eastern, Pale-headed, Blue-cheeked and Northern Rosella should measure at least 2–2.5 metres long x 1 metre wide x 1.2 metres high. Larger birds including the Crimson, Yellow and Green Rosella should be housed in aviaries measuring approximately 3–3.5 metres long x 1 metre wide x 1.2 metres high.

Conventional Aviaries

In Europe, conventional aviaries are of a similar design to Australian versions. Most European aviculturists provide their birds with year-long access to sun, shade and other external elements. Some enclosures are solid and feature a small opening to the flights so that birds may escape severe climatic conditions. Some enclosures are heated, sound-proofed and fitted with UVB lighting.

Open wire flights are common in Australia and Europe. While some European aviaries are brick structures with tiled floors and walls to make cleaning easier, most are similar to Australian designs. Although many older complexes are constructed from timber, the use of aluminium is increasing in popularity in the construction of new flights. Birds are housed in aviaries designed to allow them access to the elements all year round.

The main considerations when building a bank of conventional aviaries to accommodate rosellas are outlined below.

Aviary Size

The size of an aviary will depend on the rosella species to be accommodated. A pair of the smaller rosella species may be kept in an aviary measuring approximately 2.5–3 metres long x 80cm wide x 2.1 metres high, while the larger species—such as the Crimson, Yellow, Adelaide and Green Rosella—will require an aviary measuring approximately 4–5 metres long x 1.2 metres wide x 2.4 metres high.

Although the height of aviaries can vary, I recommend they stand approximately 2.4 metres tall. This height will increase construction costs but is associated with many advantages. Birds prefer to roost as high as possible at night and the extra height allows the perch to be placed higher—enabling most people to walk under the back perch without ducking. Importantly, it allows the sun to shine to the back of the enclosure during an Australian winter—ensuring the enclosure stays warm and dry.

When determining aviary length, consider the material being used on the internal walls—whether it is sheeting such as Zincalume®, Colorbond®, Villaboard® or fibrous cement. Design should eliminate wastage—sheeting materials are usually available in varying widths and this should be calculated in the aviary measurements. If you must cut sheets then try to utilise the off-cuts in other areas of the construction.

Many European aviary complexes are attached to indoor housing facilities and are set among attractive landscaped gardens

This bank of conventional aviaries incorporates a suspended feeding boot and perch at the front

These suspended aviaries provide easy access to feed stations and nestboxes from a rear enclosed area. Discarded waste is easily cleaned from the concrete floor below the aviary

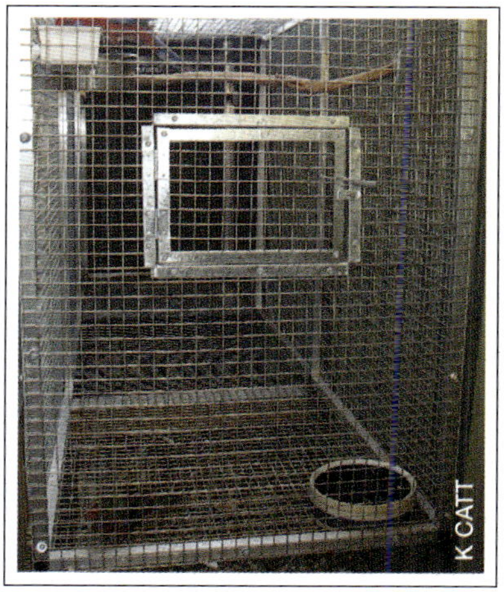

Suspended aviary

This conventional aviary incorporates a grassed substrate, a sheltered roosting and feeding area and a large open flight section allowing the birds access to the weather while also providing sufficient shade

Substrate

The most hygienic aviary floor is constructed from concrete. The advantages are that it prevents vermin, predators and other creatures entering the aviary from below and deters intestinal worms and other parasites from becoming established. Concrete is also relatively easy to clean by hose, high pressure cleaning, scraping or sweeping.

The disadvantages are the expense and difficulty in laying concrete—a professional concreter or some skilled friends might be required.

An aviary design that allows for rodent entry, discarded food build-up and an earthen substrate is a recipe for health and breeding problems

Concrete slabs are usually laid with a slight gradient to enable water run-off. Aviary floors may be designed to slope towards strategically placed drains, which must be covered to prevent vermin entering the enclosure. I place 6mm x 6mm wire mesh under the grates on the drains in my aviaries—this deters vermin while maintaining the functionality of the drain.

A concrete slab with a smooth finish will make cleaning a lot easier than a rough or textured slab. Sand or grit may be spread over the concrete to provide the birds with something to scratch around in. However, this takes more time and effort to clean and must be replaced after each cleaning.

If concrete is not desired, at the very least brick or concrete footings should be laid to support the aviary walls and to anchor the frame to the ground. The gaps between the footings should be filled with sand or gravel that can be raked over and replaced annually. This type of floor will not prevent vermin from entering the aviary—this can be achieved by digging a trench measuring approximately 20cm wide x 60cm deep around the perimeter of the cage and filling it with concrete.

At a minimum, the walkway and rear section of the aviary—where the feeding stations and the rear perch are often located—should be concreted. This will facilitate faster and easier cleaning.

Framework

Most aviary complexes are constructed using steel, although timber was very popular in the past. In my experience, the best steel frame is constructed from 20–25mm^2 galvanised RHS. Steel frames are relatively easy to fabricate and are extremely strong and durable. They can be welded together or joined by using plastic joiners.

Aluminium framework is increasing in popularity worldwide, particularly in the construction of suspended cages. Aluminium frames are light weight and can be fastened together with plastic joiners—making them easy and quick to fabricate.

Aluminium frames are light and can be joined together with plastic joiners

When constructing framework, the frame must be anchored to the foundations of the aviary complex with dynabolts—these can be purchased from any hardware store. Dynabolts are relatively easy to install and can be inserted directly into the concrete through the frame or by attaching a bracket—galvanised L-shaped brackets are most suitable—by welding to the steel frame and then bolting into the slab

Walls

Consider fully partitioning an aviary—I have achieved excellent breeding results with full partitioning. If birds cannot see other pairs they will squabble with their neighbours less and concentrate on their own mates and breeding.

A variety of materials can be used to construct the internal walls of an aviary. Colorbond® sheeting is the most suitable and should be placed along the full length of the aviary. If wire is desired for the internal walls it must, at the very minimum, be double-wired to prevent injuries to neighbouring birds.

Concrete is the most hygienic substrate—external walls should be sealed at the base to prevent entry by vermin and predators

External walls should be sealed at the base to prevent entry by vermin and predators. This can be achieved by screwing a piece of steel angle measuring approximately 25mm x 50mm to the bottom of the aviary frame. The external wall sheets are then placed on the steel angle and screwed to the frame. This should result in the bottom of the sheets sitting 25mm lower than the top of the concrete.

Roof

There are two basic aviary roofing designs—solid coverage of the shelter and the flight areas, or solid coverage of the shelter area and wire coverage of the flight area. Generally, the higher an aviary, the greater amount of roof area that needs to be solid.

A combination of steel, Zincalume® or Colorbond® and polycarbonate is suitable for solid roofed cages. If using polycarbonate be aware that while allowing extra light into the aviary increased heat is generated—a concern in warmer climates.

If a section of the aviary roof is constructed using wire, it is vital the sheltered section is of sufficient size to keep the feeding and roosting areas dry in inclement weather.

An electric fence over the roof deters wild birds from perching. Note the sprinkler system to cool the birds on hot days

Incorporating an uncovered suspended wire section to the front of the aviary keeps the fully roofed area of the aviary floor dry while allowing birds access to sun and rain

A third option—growing in popularity and one that I endorse—is to cover the entire aviary in roofing iron and incorporate a small, uncovered suspended wire section to the front of the aviary. This keeps the aviary floor dry while also allowing the birds to have access to the sun and the rain. Greenfoods such as endive, celery and milk thistle as well as apples, corn and water can be located in this 'feeding boot'. Wastage falls through the wire base onto the ground outside the aviary where it can be processed into mulch.

The installation of an electric fence is recommended on the roof of this suspended section to deter wild birds from perching on the aviary. Placement of a sprinkler system in this area will also cool the birds on hot days.

Insulation should be placed underneath the roofing iron in the rear section of the aviary—fibrous cement or Villaboard® is ideal. Insulation will cool the aviary in summer and prevent heavy condensation dripping off the underside of the iron in winter.

Walkway

The most important section of an aviary is often the walkway—located either in the front or rear of the complex. It facilitates nest inspection, regular cleaning and maintenance and can prevent the loss of a bird that has escaped through an open door of a flight.

A front walkway is generally constructed from wire and features one door—usually at one end of the aviary. This door may be solid or covered by wire. The disadvantages of a front walkway are that to view birds from outside, you must peer through two sections of wire. It can also be difficult to feed or inspect birds when entering aviaries from the front as you must approach the rear as the birds fly past. If there is insufficient space above your head this can be disastrous when newly fledged young are flying unsteadily.

Although a front walkway is less expensive and faster to construct, a rear walkway is preferable as it allows for easier servicing of the aviaries. The birds must simply fly to the front perch and wait until feeding or nest inspection is complete.

The main disadvantage of a rear walkway is that it may create drafts. However, covering the back wall of the aviary with a solid material will overcome this problem.

Various aviary designs incorporate one walkway servicing two banks of cages—one bank on either side—with access provided to the front of one cage bank and the rear of the opposite cage bank.

A suitable walkway should measure at least 80cm wide—sufficient in width to allow access for a wheelbarrow. An ideal walkway would measure approximately 1.5 metres wide. However, a walkway measuring approximately 1.2 metres is recommended—this allows for the nestbox to be positioned from the walkway with only the nest entrance protruding into the cage. A shelf or bench space where seed and accessories may be stored is a most useful addition.

This walkway is wide enough to include shelving and storage

Aviary doors should be of sufficient height to allow entry without having to duck your head and be fitted with self-closing springs to prevent the birds from escaping.

All birds are nervous at night and can be easily startled. Lights that automatically turn on as darkness approaches should be installed in the walkway to reduce night fright and bird injuries.

Ample access to feeding stations and nestboxes is available in this design

This aviary design includes an area for record keeping as well as storage

Wire

The main consideration when selecting wire for a rosella aviary should be the type of wire that will best prevent vermin and predators from entering the enclosure—rosellas do not regularly chew wire and escape.

Wire and welded mesh are available in various gauge and aperture sizes—your choice should depend on the size of your cages. Most wire is available in 900mm or 1200mm wide rolls. If your cages are 2.4 metres high, 900mm wide rolls of wire will not be suitable. Generally wire mesh measuring approximately 12mm x 25mm in aperture is suitable for all rosella species. It is best fixed to the frame using tex screws.

To reduce flight hazards for fledging birds, be aware of the aviary length when attaching wire to the front. Wire should be left slightly loose to prevent young rosellas from cracking their breastbone during flight—a particular problem when sheets of heavy gauge welded mesh are used.

Aviary wire should be manufactured from top materials to ensure it is of good quality. In Australia, local wire is superior in quality compared to less expensive, imported wire—which is generally not as square, resulting in the need to cut it into shorter lengths before fixing it to the frame.

Prior to introducing any birds into the aviary, wire must be scrubbed with a wire brush using a solution of vinegar and water to remove all zinc oxide residue and clags.

The Fit-out

Watering Systems

It is highly recommended to include a watering system in your aviary design. There are a wide variety of designs available.

In my aviaries I have placed 13mm poly pipe underneath the front suspended section of the bank. Attached to this poly pipe via a small valve is a piece of 6mm tubing—as used for garden sprinklers—placed strategically to enter the cage. To deter the birds from chewing the tubing it is encased inside a piece of 10mm copper pipe that is bent and pointed into the water bowl. The copper pipe is then anchored to the aviary frame using a saddle and tex screws.

Using this system, water bowls in all the cages of an aviary bank can be flushed out by turning on one tap. I have been able to flush out and provide fresh water to more than 80 aviaries in less than five minutes with this system. Timers can also be used to commence watering at specified times.

The Edstrom™ ball system is another water system design, popular because it is very tidy and simple to install. A water line—usually a 13mm poly pipe—is laid along the front or rear of the aviaries. From this, a smaller tube deviates with a brass ball attached to the end. This brass ball is held in position away from the wire by a clip. A bird simply pushes the ball with its beak and the water flows into its mouth. The advantages of this system are that there are no bowls to clean and water usage is kept to a minimum. However, relying solely upon this system presents a big disadvantage—the birds do not have access to a water bowl for bathing, which is important for their hygiene and general wellbeing and provides moisture for the hen to generate humidity in the nest during the breeding season.

In this watering system polypipe is run along the outside of the aviary and linked via a valve to a smaller pipe which is encased in a 10mm copper pipe that is bent and pointed into the water bowl

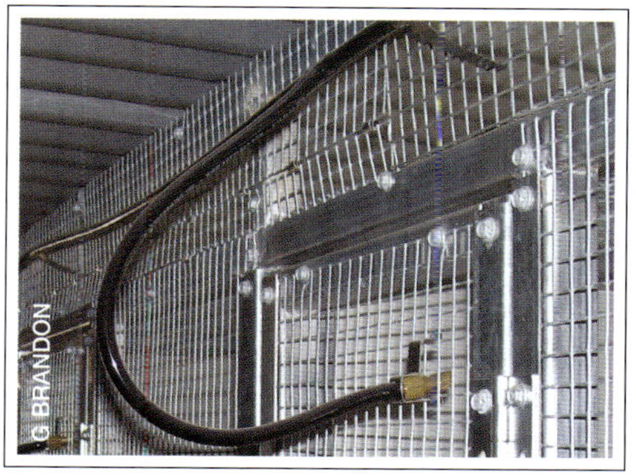

The Edstrom™ ball water system is an extremely efficient design—tidy and simple to install

This automated watering system enables all aviaries to be supplied with fresh water at once

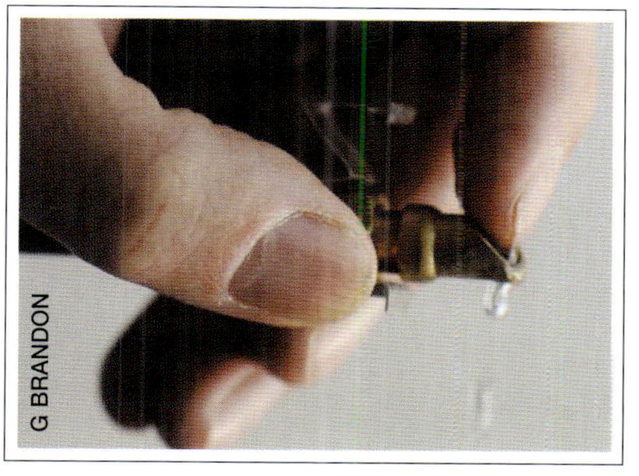

The Edstrom™ ball water system. To access water the bird pushes the ball with its beak and water flows into its mouth

Perches

Perches should be placed at either end of an aviary to maximise the flying distance. Rosella cocks have a tendency for obesity, therefore the more exercise they receive the better.

The front perch should be placed lower than the rear perch to encourage the birds to roost in the rear of the shelter—not one of my rosella pairs roost on the front perch. To prevent faecal contamination, perches should not be placed above water bowls or feed stations.

There are various methods of securing perches to the walls of an aviary. The most popular is an inexpensive, small, metal, V-shaped perch holder. These are screwed or pop-riveted to the wall—the perch is simply placed into the holders.

The late Kevin Thomson, of Thomson's Aviary Products in New South Wales, designed and manufactured perch holders that could be secured to the wall or hung on the wire. Kevin was an innovator and revolutionised many aspects of aviary furniture for Australian aviculturists—from nestbox, carry box, feed bin, swivel feeder and perch holder designs to developing the ultimate sliding feed station system. His contribution to Australian aviculture should never be underestimated.

Natural tree branches of varying shapes and diameters are suitable for use as perches as they provide exercise for birds' feet. Perches will need to be changed periodically as rosellas do chew them. Hardwood perches—such as those used as tomato stakes—are preferable to softwood perches that require replacement more frequently.

A popular method of securing perches to the aviary wall is by placing them in a V-shaped metal perch holder, pop-riveted to the wall

The introduction of new perches will provide stimulation within the aviary—rosellas will spend hours chewing the bark off. Branches may also be placed at the front of an aviary by the main perch—giving the birds a structure to climb and the opportunity to exercise.

A good friend of mine—Steve Slade, well known for his attention to detail—hangs rope from the roof of his aviaries and ties it around the middle of a branch. When a rosella lands on the perch it swings around and up and down—creating variety for the birds and a lot of laughs for Steve.

Hanging Nests

The most common method of hanging nesting logs is to attach lengths of chain or wire to the nest and to fasten these to the roof or on the sides of the aviary. Constructing a stand to place a log on within the sheltered area is also popular. However, the disadvantages of these methods are that they may trap an inquisitive rosella at the rear of a log or a bird's leg ring may become caught in the chain or wire.

A method of hanging nestboxes is to secure one 'J' bracket to the wall and another on the nestbox

A more suitable method for hanging nestboxes was developed by the late Kevin Thomson. His 'J' bracket design was constructed from a length of thin metal bent into a 'J' shape and fastened to the wall of the aviary by screws or a pop-rivet. A second 'J' bracket was placed upside down and screwed into the rear of the nestbox—locking the two 'J' sections together. A row of 'J' brackets may be secured inside walkways or birdrooms for simple, easy hanging and for the storage of nestboxes during the non-breeding season.

Feeding Stations

The locations of feeding stations and the methods of providing foods should be determined at the fit-out stage of construction. Feeding stations should be identical in each cage—it makes interchanging birds less stressful for them and the servicing of accessories much easier. It also provides the appearance of uniformity.

There are various methods of providing food. Open, glazed, ceramic bowls may be placed above floor level or on a shelf in a corner of the aviary, or seed hoppers may be located with the feeding station within the aviary. When considering the location, ensure it is clear of perches and the nestbox and that it is easy to remove, clean and replace.

In my aviary I hang a feed bin just in front of the rear perch on the wall opposite the location of the nestbox. This location prevents contamination.

The most popular method of feeding soft foods to birds is in stainless steel bowls attached to the cage. These bowls may be fastened by large rings that clip onto the wire or by small brackets that swivel the feeder bowls in and out of the cage.

The 'slider' design is an innovative feeding station comprising an aluminium frame that extends through the cage wall, or wire, and a hinged door that lifts up to allow

These feeding systems manufactured by Thomson Aviary Products provide easily accessed food bowls—simply lift the hinged door to slide-out

This seed hopper design provides a catchment area for spilt seed

Incorporate the same feeding stations in every aviary to facilitate efficient servicing and to provide a familiar aviary fit-out for birds when they are moved

access to food bowls by sliding them in and out of the cage. This is the benchmark against which all other feeding systems will be measured in the future.

When determining feeding stations, consider the placement of cuttlefish bone, calcium bells and shell grit. The design should discourage birds from fouling them or discarding them onto the floor, creating waste.

Bathing

Most rosellas love to bathe and are much more inclined to do this than hang on wire in the rain or under sprinklers—as some other species such as cockatoos or Princess Parrots prefer. I have observed birds standing in water bowls flapping their wings and fluffing their feathers even on the coldest mornings when the water is half frozen. Ensure a bowl of water is always available.

Glazed, ceramic bowls with a diameter of 200–230mm and a depth of 50–70mm are ideal. This depth will allow rosellas to get into a freshly filled bowl and splash around until it is nearly empty. With their smooth surface, ceramic bowls are easy to clean and are not prone to algae infestations.

The Birdroom

Many aviculturists incorporate a birdroom into their aviary complex to store seed, nests and carry and freight boxes. They are ideal for storing catching nets and other necessities used on a regular basis and are also a good place to place transport cages or show boxes if you attend bird sales and shows. Installation of a sink and a fridge is recommended to enable food preparation and storage. Shelves and cupboards will provide places for storing leg rings, medications, disinfectants, spare food and water bowls. Some aviculturists also store a hospital box in their birdroom for sick or injured birds.

This birdroom includes an area for food preparation, the cleaning of food equipment and storage

Other Considerations

When constructing new cages always consider the design from a bird's viewpoint. Sharp corners and pieces of wire that may cause injuries or small gaps where a leg ring may become wedged must be eliminated.

Rosellas are extremely aggressive species and should be protected from each other. They should be housed as one pair per aviary for breeding purposes. Young rosellas can be housed together in holding cages but there must be no nests available. All birds must be released into the aviary at the same time—a new bird introduced at a later date will be attacked by the existing birds and either killed or harassed until it dies of exhaustion.

Before releasing any birds into their newly constructed home, the aviary should be cleaned thoroughly and hosed out to remove any metal filings and cement dust.

Aviaries should be as easy to maintain and clean as possible. It is worth putting extra time, effort and thought into the design process to achieve this.

FEEDING

The feeding of birds is one of the most important aspects in caring for and breeding any parrot species, including rosellas. Knowledge on the feeding requirements of birds and the nutritional value of most foods has increased significantly in recent years. There is now no excuse for feeding birds just seed and water—a diet deficient in nutritional content. There are a large variety of commercial diets and manufactured pelleted foods currently available to aviculturists—as well as vitamin and mineral supplements, breeding tonics, special seed mixes and sprouting mixes. However, birds may overdose on some nutrients if excess supplements are provided—especially in conjunction with a nutritionally balanced pelleted diet.

Rosellas, such as this Northern Rosella relish seeding grasses

Aviculturists with small collections—10 pairs of parrots or less—are able to supply generous quantities of a wide food selection—but the birds do not necessarily receive extra benefits from this diet. Generally, more wastage is generated when birds are fed greater quantities. I recommend only feeding birds what they can eat in a day—anything more is wasted and may increase your financial outlay as well as the time required to clean up the discarded food. However, the amount and variety of food on offer should be increased during the breeding season—especially when there are young in the nest.

Rosellas with young in the nest require copious amounts of food to successfully rear all of their chicks. An insufficient supply of food to the parent birds at this critical stage is the main reason chicks die in the nest—particularly the youngest chicks. These younger, smaller chicks only have to miss one or two feeds through lack of food to die.

Sprouted seeds and vegetables provide essential vitamins and minerals not present in an all-seed diet

As a bird collection grows, so does the time required to feed and care for them. The diet you offer your birds must be relatively easy to prepare. A complicated feeding routine and a large number of aviaries to service can easily become too difficult and time consuming—and may result in attempts to rush, whereby feeds can be missed and the birds will subsequently suffer.

For rosellas that breed in spring, special breeding diets should commence in July and the variety and quantity of food offered increased. For winter breeding birds, this routine should be commenced close to the beginning of March. To achieve maximum fertility in birds by September—when they are due to mate and lay eggs—add calcium and a vitamin and mineral powder to a sprouted seed and vegetable mix and increase the amount of greenfood.

After the chicks hatch, this balanced diet should be maintained for the parents and the amount of food increased as the chicks develop. This is a particularly important aspect of successful breeding. For a pair of birds to successfully rear five or six young they must be supplied with sufficient food—during the growing stage chicks will consume more food than an adult bird.

From my breeding experience I recommend the following routine:

- During the breeding season feed the birds twice a day—morning and afternoon—to maximise the chances of successfully rearing all chicks. Offer the birds a sprouted seed and vegetable mix in the morning. In the afternoon, provide greenfood, apple and corn. It does not necessarily matter in which order the food is offered—as long as the birds are supplied with the right types of food and in sufficient quantities.
- During the non-breeding season reduce the diet and its nutritional content to ensure the birds are receiving a more basic maintenance diet. Provide the sprouted seed and vegetable mix once or twice a week and increase the quantity of celery. Celery is an excellent form of greenfood to offer young growing rosellas. They devour it with great enthusiasm—a dozen or more rosellas will consume two or three sticks of celery in just a few hours.

Seed Diet

Dry seed is the most common base diet for rosellas. Combined with a variety of fresh fruits and vegetables—in particular greenfoods—and a good sprouted seed mix, it will provide birds with a balanced diet that will keep them healthy and encourage them to breed successfully.

Although some aviculturists are embracing pelleted diets, it is doubtful they will become as popular in Australia as they are overseas.

I feed all rosellas in my collection the same seed mix—10% sunflower, 10% safflower, 35% canary, 30% millets, 10% hulled oats and 5% mixed canola and linseed. This may appear a little light on sunflower seed, but I have found it very effective over the past 15 years.

Fewer 'oilseeds'—such as sunflower, safflower, linseed, canola and niger—high in fat and low in carbohydrates—should be fed. Greater quantities of millets and cereal grains are a healthier option. Rosellas can suffer with obesity—particularly cocks of the larger Green, Crimson and Adelaide Rosella species—and this must be monitored. An overweight rosella cock will find it difficult to copulate and fertilise eggs.

The quality of a seed mix is a large part of a successful breeding program. Seed used must be clean and graded—the extra cost is a worthy investment.

When selecting seed from a supplier for the first time, take a sample home and sprout it. A sprouting rate of less than 90% is unacceptable. If the seed does not sprout it is either dead or has not developed during the growing stage and therefore has no nutritional content. Aviculturists who experience poor breeding results, and cannot understand why, should perhaps examine the sprouting rate of their seed—it may answer a few questions.

Pelleted Diet

Pelleted diets have been available in Australia since the early 1990s. Although they are often promoted as a complete diet, the actual benefits remain a topic of debate. Despite manufacturer's claims to the contrary, wastage is not avoided with a pelleted diet—dust and powder from the pellets will drop on the aviary floor as the pellets are eaten. Some pelleted diets can be relatively expensive.

If feeding pelleted diets, provide a variety of fruits, vegetables and a seed mix for variety

Regardless of opinion, pelleted diets have changed significantly over the past decade and new products continue to be developed. Pellet textures, shapes and colours have all improved and some aviculturists may find it beneficial to introduce this food source to their birds. I suggest that birds be offered a varied diet throughout the year—different tastes, sizes, textures and smells—otherwise they may become bored with any diet.

When pelleted foods were first released in Australia I converted several pairs of birds including rosellas, Princess Parrots, King Parrots and cockatoos to this diet. During the 3–4 week conversion process, I eliminated all other food sources including seed, greenfoods and sprouts. When any of these foods were added, the birds ceased eating the pellets and would gorge themselves on greenfoods or sprouts—refusing the pellets for a day or more.

During the damp and wet winter period, heavy fogs would often cause the pellets to soften and become mouldy. Therefore, the supply was limited to last two days maximum.

During spring, some pairs of the birds on this diet—rosella and Princess Parrots—bred. Their chicks were headreared from 10 days of age and weaned on commercial crumbles, then pellets. They continually begged for food and always preferred greenfood over pellets—leaving the pellets untouched until all of the greenfood was consumed. At approximately three months of age the birds were introduced to a seed diet. All of the birds in the cage went straight to the bowl containing the seed mix—consisting of sunflower, safflower, canary and some millet seeds—and gorged themselves—a staggering result. They cracked and consumed the seed as if they had not eaten in days and as if they were veterans. After two days I removed all of the pelleted food and provided mixed seeds and a variety of fruits and vegetables.

Presently I feed some of my exotic parrot species a pelleted diet combined with fruits and vegetables. I do not know of any aviculturists who feed a solely pelleted diet to rosellas.

Sprouting Seed

In the wild, birds generally feed on ripened or half ripened seed heads and will travel long distances from their nests to feeding grounds. During the return journey, the seed digests and softens in the adult crop before it is fed to the chicks. For obvious reasons this process is not possible with captive birds.

Sprouted seed has been a popular food source for captive birds for a number of years as it is a highly nutritious source of proteins and vitamins for parent birds to feed to their chicks. The protein and vitamin content of dry seed increases significantly when it sprouts. And when soaked, sprouted seed is softer and more easily digested than dry seed. Often as soon as parent birds consume sprouts they are back in the nest feeding their chicks.

A basic sprouting mix consists of sunflower and safflower seeds, mung beans, lupins, sorghum and barley. Maize, chickpeas, dun peas, wheat and a small quantity of pigeon

Sprouted seed is a highly nutritious source of protein and vitamins for parent birds to feed to their chicks. The protein and vitamin content of dry seed increases significantly when it sprouts. Fruits and vegetables are added to sprouted seeds (on the right) and provided daily to breeding birds

mix can be added along with blue peas, black-eyed beans, cannellini (Great Northern) beans and soybeans.

To prepare the mix, place the ingredients into a stainless steel colander and rinse with water. Next, transfer into a large stainless steel mixing bowl where the seed mixture should be soaked in fresh water for approximately 12 hours. Rinse thoroughly in water, drain and place in a warm location for 24–48 hours—depending on the room temperature. Rinse the sprouting seed in water once or twice a day during this period—until it has sprouted sufficiently—3–4mm long is ideal. Discard any rancid seed during the process.

Another option is the use of a 'hot box' in which to sprout seed. Such a box was designed and constructed by respected rosella breeder Laurie Arnold. The idea behind the 'hot box' design is that, under a controlled temperature, the seed will sprout faster—reducing the risk of it becoming rancid and growing mould. The turnaround time between batches is also much faster.

Laurie constructed his box from coolroom panelling—the original design was large enough to warm a baby elephant! I adapted Laurie's design to a slightly smaller scale. Constructed from 13mm melamine sheeting, it is fitted with 25mm^2 weldmesh shelves and two light globes installed in the base—a thermostat controls the temperature. Soaked seed is placed in the 'hot box' overnight and rinsed early the next morning. Approximately 24 hours later the seed is ready for feeding. This method of sprouting is faster and safer than natural sprouting. Using conventional sprouting methods, the seed can take 2–3 days to sprout during winter, which may increase the risk of spoiling.

Bad seed can be identified much faster in a 'hot box' compared with conventional sprouting. I have observed sunflower seed growing mould in a 'hot box' after only six to eight hours. When this seed was sprouted using conventional methods it appeared normal—approximately 60% sprouted.

The 'hot box' design facilitates the seed to sprout faster—reducing the risks of rancidity and mould

Upon investigation I observed that the mould-covered seed was rotten inside. All of this suspect seed was discarded. It is vital to always use clean, good quality graded seed.

Contrary to popular practice, I do not use any bleach or cleanser during the sprouting process and I have never had any trouble with seed spoiling—apart from the case mentioned in the previous paragraph.

Fruits and Vegetables

Rosellas will eat a wide variety of fruits and vegetables—provided these food items have been introduced into their diet at an early age. It is much more difficult to entice older birds to sample new foods than it is to tempt younger birds with new foods—young birds will eat virtually anything you offer them. If one bird in a holding cage commences eating a particular foodstuff, the rest will follow.

Diced fruits and vegetables and sprouted seed can be sprinkled with a nutritional supplement

I feed my rosellas celery, endive, apples, corn, carrots, peas, beans and potato—either diced in a bowl and mixed with sprouted seed or cut into larger pieces and placed on a tray. Silverbeet, pumpkin, papaya, watermelon, pear, grapes, tomatoes, orange, pomegranate, kiwifruit, brussel sprouts, kale, brown rice, leak, chickpeas, pumpkin seeds, broccoli, red pepper, sweet potato, squash, asparagus, lentils, turnip, cauliflower, banana, cabbage, cucumber, berries, nuts and parsley may also be offered—as well as Madeira cake, wholemeal bread, egg and biscuit mix and hard boiled eggs.

Seeding Grasses and Native Foods

A variety of seeding grasses and weeds may be offered to rosellas—such as milk thistle, dandelion, millet spray, chickweed, dock, shepherd's purse, rye grass, couch grass, Johnson grass and winter grass.

Also consumed by rosellas are gum nuts and flowers, hawthorn, callistemon, *Grevillia* spp, *Hakea* spp, *Leptospermum* spp, *Melaleuca* spp, *Acacia* spp, and cotoneaster berries.

Wintergrass

Milk thistle

Chickweed

Miscellaneous Food Sources

I have never supplied meat or chicken bones to any rosella—I did offer them to cockatoo pairs but ceased the practice as it attracted a large number of ants.

Smaller rosellas will not generally eat mealworms but I have observed the Crimson, Adelaide and Yellow Rosella species accept them—I see no reason why the Green Rosella would not also.

Some rosellas will accept fly pupae—an excellent source of protein.

Various shell and charcoal grits, cuttlebone and calcium blocks are essential dietary items

Throughout the year, good quality shell grits and cuttlefish bone or calcium blocks with charcoal added should be made available. Although breeding hens may not touch the calcium blocks during the non-breeding season, by August they will generally start to chew it.

NUTRITIONAL REQUIREMENTS

Vitamins and Minerals

Vitamin A

Vitamin A aids in healthy vision, optimum bone growth, immune system function, protection from viral infections, growth and development of bones and reproduction.

Vitamin A is found in carrot, spinach, kale, red pepper, sweet potato, squash, broccoli, tomato, asparagus, beans, peas, celery, orange and endive.

Vitamin B1 (Thiamine)

Vitamin B1 is the major provider of fuel in a body—maintaining energy, coordinating nerves and muscles, supporting heart function and assisting in the maintenance of appetite.

Vitamin B1 is found in sunflower seed, black bean, peas, lentils, corn, spinach, celery, tomato, red pepper, carrot, squash, kale and brussel sprouts.

Cooking can reduce Vitamin B1 content by up to 90% in some foods.

Vitamin B2 (Riboflavin)

Vitamin B2 plays an essential role in the metabolic activity of the liver and kidneys and supports energy production. It assists in cell function and skin and feather quality.

Vitamin B2 is found in soybean, spinach, broccoli, asparagus, turnip, boiled eggs, celery, kale, beans, tomato and peas.

Although cooking and storage has little effect on levels of vitamin B2 in foods, prolonged exposure to light can greatly reduce nutritional quality.

Vitamin B3 (Niacin)

Vitamin B3 supports genetic processes in the cells, stabilising blood sugar and aiding in fat metabolism, skin and feather quality.

Vitamin B3 is found in asparagus, tomato, squash, peas, carrot, broccoli, peanuts, spinach, kale and beans.

Vitamin B5 (Pantothenic Acid)

Vitamin B5 converts carbohydrates and fats into usable energy. It supports the adrenal glands, feather development and the maintenance of a healthy digestive tract.

Vitamin B5 is found in sunflower seed, corn, broccoli, squash, turnip, tomato, boiled eggs, cauliflower and silverbeet.

Vitamin B6 (Pyridoxine)

Vitamin B6 supports the function of the nervous system, general metabolism, feather and skin growth and stimulates the appetite. Deficiencies in vitamin B6 can cause decreased growth rates, a decline in egg production and poor egg hatchability.

Vitamin B6 is found in banana, spinach, red pepper, turnip, peas, celery, broccoli, kale, cabbage, tomato, carrot and sweet potato.

Cooking and freezing these foods greatly reduces their nutritional value.

Biotin

Biotin affects egg hatchability and supports metabolic functions and bone formation.

Biotin is found in almonds, egg, cabbage, cucumber, cauliflower, berries and nuts.

Vitamin C

Vitamin C aids healing by boosting the immune system and preventing cell damage and improves iron absorption.

Vitamin C is found in papaya, red pepper, orange, kiwifruit, broccoli, carrot, celery, kale, cauliflower, cabbage, tomato, spinach, beans, apple, peas, corn and endive.

Foods containing vitamin C are most effective when consumed raw.

Vitamin D3

Vitamin D3 is essential for bone and cell development, maintenance of the immune system, in the prevention of soft-shelled eggs, egg-binding and Rickets. It assists in the absorption of calcium.

Vitamin D3 is found in boiled egg and fish oils. Exposure to direct sunlight also increases levels of vitamin D3.

Vitamin E

Vitamin E aids in the absorption of nutrients, in blood circulation and increases fertility. Its effectiveness is closely related to levels of vitamin C, selenium, glutathione and vitamin B3. Vitamin E deficiencies can lead to problems with the nervous system, low egg hatchability and infertility.

Vitamin E is found in sunflower seed, silverbeet, almonds, spinach, parsley, kale, papaya, olives, pepper, brussel sprouts, kiwifruit, tomato, broccoli and wheat germ.

Vitamin K

Vitamin K is essential to normal blood clotting and aids the function of the digestive system and the liver and supports the maintenance of strong and healthy bones.

Vitamin K is found in spinach, silverbeet, celery, brussel sprouts, peas, beans, asparagus, broccoli, kale, endive and carrot.

Calcium

Calcium is essential for the maintenance of strong and healthy bones, feather development and aids in normal blood clotting and healthy functioning of the nervous system. It is vital in the development of eggshells—calcium reduces egg-binding and the production of soft-shelled eggs in hens and Rickets in young birds.

Calcium is found in spinach, sesame seeds, broccoli, fennel, squash, beans, orange, brussel sprouts, silverbeet, celery, kale, basil, thyme and dill seeds.

Chlorine

Chlorine is essential in maintaining balanced acid and alkaline levels in the gut and aids in digestion.

Chlorine is found in shell grit and salt.

Iron

Iron is essential to the distribution of oxygen via the blood, in energy production and assists in the function of a healthy immune system. Birds deficient in iron will be lethargic and more susceptible to infections. Birds suffering from parasitic infections may need extra iron in their diet—parasites withdraw blood reducing iron levels.

Iron is found in silverbeet, spinach, thyme, beans, lentils, brussel sprouts, asparagus, broccoli, kale, leak and endive.

Magnesium

Magnesium plays an essential role in the functioning of the nervous system, genes and muscles, aiding in the strength and development of bones, and in the metabolism of fats, proteins and carbohydrates.

Magnesium is found in pumpkin seeds, spinach, silverbeet, soybean, sunflower and sesame seeds, almond, peanuts, squash, broccoli, cucumber, beans, celery and kale.

Manganese

Manganese complements the action of other key minerals and activates enzymes. It assists in the development of strong and healthy bones and muscles, growth and reproduction.

Manganese is found in pineapple, brown rice, spinach, chickpeas, whole grains, soybean, turnip, silverbeet, kale, grapes, squash, peas, berries, carrot, corn and celery.

Protein

Protein plays an important role in the reproduction of enzymes and is essential for feather development. It also contributes to the effective function of the immune system, growth and development.

Protien is found in broccoli, kale, boiled eggs, lentils, brussel sprouts, peanuts, whole grains, beans, asparagus, spinach, soybeans, peas and silverbeet.

Cystine

Cystine is an essential amino acid and one of the building blocks of protein. It is required for optimum feather growth in young developing chicks and moulting adult parrots. Low levels of cystine may result in reduced function of the immune system.

Cystine is found in eggs, red pepper, broccoli, brussel sprouts, oats and wheat germ.

Lysine

Lysine is another essential amino acid and a building block of protein. It aids in the absorption of calcium and muscle development—required for optimum bone development in young birds. Lysine deficiencies can cause reproductive problems.

Lysine is found in nuts, egg, soybeans and legumes such as beans, peas and lentils.

Beta-carotene

β-carotene, a precursor to vitamin A, plays an important role in the protection of cells and the functioning of the immune and reproductive systems.

β-carotene is found in sweet potato, carrot, kale, spinach, turnip, squash, thyme and broccoli. Endive—one of the most popular greenfoods fed to rosellas in Australia—is a major source of β-carotene. Note that Australian endive, commonly named 'curly endive', is different to the endive derived from the root of the Chicory plant in the USA and Europe.

Nutritional Composition of Grains

The following table outlines the levels of protein, fat, carbohydrate, fibre and kilojoules of common Australian grains fed to rosellas.

	Protein	Fat	Fibre	Carbohydrate	Energy (kJ)
	In Grams per 100 Grams				
SEEDS					
French White millet	13	2	9	62	n/a
Panorama	13	3	9	59	1460
Japanese millet	15	6	11	60	1490
Panicum	11	4	7	63	1480
Canary	14	3	21	56	1360
OIL SEEDS					
Grey-striped Sunflower	23	41	11	17	2395
Safflower	14	44	31	16	n/a
Canola (rape)	20	47	6	19	2420
Niger	19	43	14	17	2500
Linseed	18	42	28	29	2230
CEREALS					
Wheat	12	2	12	71	1510
Oats	17	7	11	66	1630
Sorghum	11	3	2	70	n/a
Corn	3	1	3	70	360
Peas	24	1	6	57	n/a

International Dietary Examples

It is interesting to note the similarities between the diets provided below and—more importantly—the differences. There are a broad variety of foods including seed mixes fed to rosellas in various countries of the world. The greatest difference between Australian and European diets is the focus on providing manufactured eggfood in Europe.

The following are examples of rosella diets fed by various aviculturists around the world:

The greatest difference between Australian and European diets is the provision of eggfood in Europe

Diet One
Supplied by Siegfried and Sabine Wiek, Germany

Seeds
This mix consists of canary seed, peeled oats, Yellow millet, Japanese millet, safflower, White millet, buckwheat, paddy rice, niger seed, milo (sorghum), linseed and sunflower seeds. Wild seeding grasses, corn on the cob and oats may also be added.

Sprouts
Developed by Versele Laga™, this sprouting seed mix is combined with small pigeon food, mixed seeds, oats and sunflower seeds.

Eggfood
Eggfood available from CEDE™, Orlux™, Wittemolen™ and Biovit™ is preferred. For best results, it is mixed with Matzinger Bio™ dried dogwood flakes, hard-boiled eggs and oat flakes.

Fruits and Vegetables
This mix consists of carrot, apple, chard, Swiss chard, dandelion, chickweed, pine seed, orange, buckwheat, garden cress and bird chalk (a type of lime).

Branches
Beech and birch branches and budding fruit tree branches are all supplied.

Supplements
Basic vitamin, mineral and amino acid supplements are mixed with the seeds and/or the eggfood.

Diet Two
Supplied by Pascal Tellier, France

Seeds
This mix comprises 20% Yellow millet, 10% White millet, 10% canary seed, 8% each of grey-striped sunflower seeds and granules, 7% peeled oats, 6% safflower seed, 5% each of Red and Saracen millet and 2% crushed oyster shells, 1% niger seed and 3% each of Japanese millet, safflower, paddy rice, hemp, linseed and wheat. Seeding grasses such as dandelion, plantain, buckwheat and other wild herbs are also offered.

Sprouts
Sprouted seeds and soaked seed mixes from Orlux™ and Versele-Laga™ are provided during the breeding season.

Fruit and Vegetables
This mix consists of a variety of fresh fruit and vegetables including apple, pear, orange, banana, carrots, red beets, pepper, gourds and broccoli.

Branches
Branches of hawthorn, Mountain Ash, sapwood, willow, hazelnut and Austrian pine trees are supplied.

Supplements
Mineral and clay blocks and cuttlefish bones are preferred.

Diet Three
Supplied by Melinda Schmitz, southern California, USA

Seeds
This mix consists of safflower, sunflower, Omaline™—a food fed to small calves—Stockbuilder™—a red pellet fortified with vitamins and minerals—Red, White and Yellow millets, oats, turkey crumbles, crushed oyster shells, buckwheat, cracked corn, wheat and canary mix.

Sprouts
Sprouted seeds including safflower, mixed frozen vegetables (thawed) and cornbread are provided during the breeding season along with seeding grasses.

Diet Four
Supplied by Roger Meuris, Belgium

Seeds

This mix varies in its composition depending on the time of year—breeding or non-breeding (winter) season. See table below:

Seed types	Breeding Season %	Non-breeding Season %
White Canary	25	20
White millet	12	18
Yellow millet	12	18
Red millet	2	2
Japanese millet	4	4
Niger	3	2
Hemp	3	2
Safflower	5	4
Buckwheat	5	7
Rice	4	4
Oats	7	5
Wheat	2	2
Flax seed	2	2
White milo	2	2
Sunflower	12	8

Eggfood

Orlux™ eggfood is mixed with insects and fruit at a ratio of 50/50 and combined with Orlux Gold Patee™ eggfood, which contains natural honey. This eggfood mixture is offered during the breeding season along with apples, carrots or broccoli three times a week. When young birds are present it is fed daily.

A sprouted seed mix consisting of mung beans, White and Yellow millets, wheat, safflower, canary seed and rice is offered three times a week mixed with eggfood and maize.

Supplements

One teaspoon of vitamin supplement Vigoramine™ per 500 grams of eggfood is provided twice a week. Once a week apple vinegar—which balances the pH of the digestive system—is included in the eggfood in 25ml per 500 grams of eggfood. Also once a week, the calcium preparation Calci-lux™ is added for the prevention and treatment of calcium deficiencies.

At the conclusion of the breeding and moulting season eggfood is offered once a week—mixed with vitamin and calcium supplements one week and with apple vinegar the next week.

Calcium, vitamin and mineral supplements are added to the eggfood diet in the pre-breeding season by Belgium breeder, Roger Meuris

BREEDING

Compatibility and Bonding

The pair bond is not as strong in some rosella species as it is in other parrot species and I have never encountered much difficulty swapping Eastern, Western, Pale-headed and Blue-cheeked Rosella partners.

Compatibility is very important to successfully breed and rear all rosella species. It is a major factor when pairing the larger Crimson, Yellow, Adelaide and Green Rosella species. Incompatible pairs of Eastern, Western, Pale-headed and Blue-cheeked Rosellas will breed, however the outcome is generally less successful—only 1–2 fertile eggs or chicks being raised. I am aware of Crimson and Adelaide Rosella cocks that were offered up to six hens before finally accepting one to settle and breed with.

Compatibility is essential to successful breeding, particularly with the larger species

It is recommended to introduce pairs at as young an age as possible to improve compatibility. There are a variety of methods to achieve this. Some aviculturists place cocks and hens in adjacent cages. If a pair appears to be spending a lot of time together or hanging onto the adjoining wire of the two cages, they can be relocated to a single breeding aviary. Another method to achieve a compatible pair is to place the cock into a cage with two or three hens and observe them for several weeks to see which hen the cock is attracted to. When this is evident relocate the other hens.

I witnessed a unique display of compatibility when I housed a young handreared hen that had only recently been weaned—with a mature cock to form a breeding pair. During close observation—mostly for any sign of aggression from the cock—I witnessed the cock feeding the hen by the end of the first day. This may have been a sign of courtship or parental display—however the pair went on to breed successfully and produced numerous young over the following years.

I have also observed young cocks feeding mature hens while housed together in holding cages—a sign of compatibility. Such pairs are placed into breeding cages. Another positive indicator of compatibility occurs when a cock sits on the nestbox or spends a lot of time peering into the nest when the hen is inside. This indicates a particularly strong pair bond leading to successful breeding outcomes.

By taking a few basic steps to encourage pair bonding and compatibility, you will generally reduce the likelihood of any breeding problems and experience success with any of the rosella species.

Courtship

The courtship display by rosellas is similar among all rosella species. The cock will stand erect and high on the perch, square his shoulders, puff out his chest and chatter loudly while wagging his tail from side-to-side and bobbing his head. This courtship display is similar in the hen, but slightly subdued in comparison to the cock.

During courtship, pairs will fly and feed together. The cock will feed the hen immediately after feeding himself. Generally, cocks are more boisterous during courtship and will spend long periods flying around the aviary, hanging onto the aviary front wire, calling and chattering loudly.

Some cocks will commence feeding the hen before nests are introduced and, in strongly bonded pairs, cocks may feed the hen throughout the year.

A Crimson Rosella cock wagging his tail in a display of courtship

Breeding Season

In Australia, the breeding season commences at the beginning of September for the Eastern, Crimson, Adelaide, Western, Yellow, Pale-headed and Green Rosellas and at the beginning of March for the Northern and Blue-cheeked Rosellas.

In the Northern Hemisphere the seasons are reversed, with spring commencing in March.

Nesting Logs and Nestboxes

Rosella hens will accept vertical or sloping nests—they do not tend to jump into the nest as some other parrot species do—therefore, the nest orientation is not critical.

Most aviculturists prefer man-made nestboxes to nesting logs as it can be difficult to find suitable logs—particularly in Europe. Nestboxes are also simple to handle, clean, store and hang in the aviary and are easier to inspect than logs. However, difficult pairs of larger rosellas—such as the Yellow, Crimson, Adelaide and Green Rosellas—may prefer a large log, particularly in Australia where they can be more difficult to breed than in Europe.

Nest Location

The nest design and location is generally not overly critical to breeding success. Nests can be located on the side of the aviary at one end, on the rear wall or in the walkway with the entrance protruding into the aviary. I have had success with boxes hung at various heights ranging from close to the roof to as low as waist-height. It is best to locate the nest at a height allowing for easy inspection without the aid of a stool or step or the need to lift the nest down. If a nest is placed high and close to the aviary roof, ensure it does not become too hot in warm temperatures.

There are some individuals that can be more particular about nest location. Flighty hens may not accept nestboxes hung at the rear of the aviary, particularly next to a walkway door. Any disturbance may distract them from breeding or, if they do nest, they may become so flighty that they flee the nest hurriedly—scattering eggs or chicks—when you enter the walkway. Some of the larger rosella species can also be particular about location—place several nests to allow the birds to select the most suitable. Unused nests can be removed—although the provision of multiple nests throughout the breeding season allows the hen to choose a different nest for a second clutch.

When deciding on nest placement, consider the overall aviary design and the location of the feeding station and water bowls.

Nest Introduction

I have always believed that the introduction of the nestbox or nesting log into the aviary plays a significant role in stimulating successful breeding in captive-bred rosellas. I recommend introducing them at the onset of spring and removing them at the end of the breeding season. If nests are left in the aviary all year round or located too early in the breeding season the first clutch can be infertile. Rosella hens generally come into breeding condition earlier than cocks and can start laying eggs without mating if they are in breeding condition. Therefore, I generally wait until the onset of spring before placing nests in the aviaries. This ensures the cock is in breeding condition and that fertility rates will be around 90 per cent in the first clutch.

In Australia, the ideal time for nest introduction is around the beginning of September for the Eastern, Crimson, Adelaide, Western, Yellow, Green and Pale-headed and at the beginning of March for the Northern and Blue-cheeked Rosella species. In warmer regions most aviculturists introduce nests earlier—generally around the middle of July or the beginning of August. I have held pairs of Pale-headed Rosellas that have nested at the same time as Northern and Blue-cheeked Rosellas and other pairs that have bred in spring.

Heating

In the colder climates in some regions of Australia and Europe nestboxes may require heating to ensure the chicks do not succumb to the cold. In Australia, daytime temperatures can rise above 30°C in the middle of spring and plummet at night. If the hen has stopped sitting at night the chicks can become chilled and die. This occurs more frequently than people realise.

An example of how to heat nestboxes

The most simple and inexpensive method of heating nests is through the installation of a low wattage (15-watt or 25-watt) light globe—located inside a can fixed to the bottom of the nestbox. This fixture can be set to turn on at night using a timer or a thermostat.

Another method is to install a heat strip—a section of insulated cable that can be cut to length to determine the wattage and, therefore, the desired temperature. This can be more expensive and is less popular than using the light globe method.

Nestboxes in Europe are generally constructed from much thicker timber than the timber used in Australia. This undoubtedly improves insulation and keeps chicks warm.

A 15-watt globe placed inside a can located at the bottom of the nestbox serves as an inexpensive method of heating

Entrance Hole

The entrance hole to a nestbox is a vital part of the nest design. If a hole is too large it will allow too much light to flow in and the hen will not feel secure enough to breed. If an entrance hole is too small the hen will have difficulty entering the nest and—depending on what material the nestbox is constructed from—she may not be able to chew her way through. I have provided nesting logs for Northern and Blue-cheeked Rosellas that had an entrance hole measuring only 50mm wide x 75mm long and cut into the top of the log—hens had to turn sideways to enter and exit.

A wooden spout fixed to the outside of the nestbox is an ideal entrance hole for rosellas. Spouts can be man-made from the same material used to construct the nestbox or constructed using a section of hollow limb—a 'natural spout'—fixed to the outside of the box.

Spouts do not allow too much light into the nest providing a secure environment for the sitting hen. Spouts also provide the cock with somewhere to perch when feeding the hen—she simply sits in the spout while the cock sits on the top and feeds her, eliminating the need for her to leave the nest.

Entrance holes—a 'natural spout' made from a section of hollow limb is fixed to the outside of the box

Examples of nestbox designs incorporating entrance holes and inspection doors

Inspection Door

All nests should include an inspection door—whether they are nestboxes or nesting logs—allowing inspection without lifting a nestbox or nesting log down. Incorporating an inspection door results in less disturbance to the hen—even the most flighty hen will return to the nest when inspection is complete.

Inspection doors should be located to minimise disruption. If the nest is hung on the outside of the aviary in the walkway, the inspection door should be located at the back of the nest. If the nest is hung on the left side of the aviary, the inspection door should be located on the left side of the nest and vice versa if the nest is hung on the right side of the aviary.

Nestbox Lid

Australian aviculturists prefer a removable lid on the nestbox, rather than a fixed lid fitted to the top. A removable lid makes it much easier to access the nestbox for cleaning and changing nest material. During higher summer temperatures, the lid can be moved to one side to allow hot air in the nestbox to escape. In extreme temperatures—to prevent the chicks from overheating—it can be completely removed and the nestbox placed on the aviary floor. As the evening temperature cools, the nestbox can be rehung with or without the lid—depending on the size and number of chicks in the nest and the temperature.

Parent birds are generally tolerant of nest relocation and will continue to feed and care for young, irrespective of where the nest is located.

Nestbox Ladder

There are two main ladder designs used in rosella nestboxes. The first design is a wire ladder that is nailed or stapled to the inside of the nestbox. It can be constructed from any wire used in the aviary construction. This ladder assists the hen when entering and exiting the nestbox—preventing her from jumping in and breaking the eggs or squashing the chicks.

The second ladder design is constructed from small pieces of wood—measuring approximately 15mm square x 50mm long. These wooden pieces are glued onto the inside of the box approximately 30–50mm apart. I prefer this design, as the hen often likes to chew the wood, which may stimulate breeding—hens can often be heard chewing on wooden ladders when preparing the nest for laying and when they are sitting on eggs and rearing chicks. Chewed ladders should be replaced at the start of the next breeding season.

This wire ladder is stapled to the inside of the nestbox

Nest Materials

Hardwood Sawdust

This material is excellent for use in rosella nests and packs down in the bottom of the nest well. It is not hard—therefore it will not chip or break the eggs—and will maintain moisture for the successful hatching of eggs. However, it is not readily available and may be difficult to source.

Peatmoss

This is the most popular nesting material used by Australian parrot breeders and is generally used in a mixture with other materials such as hardwood sawdust or woodshavings. Moisture retention is excellent, it is soft and it combines well with most other nesting materials. It is available from most garden outlets.

Wood Shavings

This material should be combined with other materials. It should not be used solely—it is very light and does not pack down into the nest well—eggs and chicks can be easily buried in the shavings under a sitting hen. Untreated wood shavings can be purchased at most produce stores.

Example of a nest base used by European aviculturists

Equal quantities of beech wood chips and hemp straw is a popular nesting material in Europe

Equal quantities of eucalypt and peatmoss is a popular nesting material in Australia

Pine Bark

This material is increasing in popularity and is available in two grades—coarse and fine. The fine grade is a by-product of pine tree plantations and is the most suitable for rosella nests. Rosella hens will chew the small pieces of bark to make a suitable nest lining. Suitability is further enhanced when mixed with peatmoss. Pine bark can be purchased from garden nurseries.

Eucalypt Mulch

This nesting material is similar to pine bark and ideal when mixed with peatmoss. It is designed for the garden landscape market in a range of decorative mulches.

Garden Soil

Small amounts of garden soil can be added to nesting material to provide it with extra substance. However, it should not contain rocks or pebbles that could break the eggs.

Natural Decayed Timber

Although wild birds use decaying material sourced from the base of trees in their nests, it is not suitable nesting material for captive birds. I know an Australian aviculturist who introduced Psittacine Beak and Feather Disease in his aviaries via material introduced from infected wild nests. He lost most of his parrots as a result.

European aviculturists use similar nesting materials to those used in Australia. Small wood chips from beech, pine or eik (oak) trees and ground hemp straw is a popular mixture. Commercial materials are also used—including the material manufactured for hamster breeding.

Changing Nest Material

During the breeding season nest material should be changed regularly. Although some nests will only need changing after the chicks have fledged, others will require changing every 4–5 days because of the amount of moisture generated from the chicks' droppings.

I have observed some Eastern Rosella hens that started to lay their second clutch of eggs before the first clutch of chicks had fledged. This scenario makes changing the nest material extremely difficult—occasionally I leave the hens alone and do not change the material until after the second clutch of chicks have hatched.

When changing the nest material, place the chicks in a plastic bucket filled with the same material as is in the nest. Move the old nest material into another bucket and replace it with fresh, pre-mixed material. Finally, move the chicks back into the fresh nest.

Nest Inspection

Nest inspection is essential to the successful rearing of rosella chicks. Numerous problems may arise during a breeding season that can be quickly identified and rectified by a simple nest inspection during the incubation and rearing stages.

It is recommended to develop a routine of inspecting nests regularly using the same process each time. A couple of taps on the side of the nest and some words or a whistle will generally be sufficient for the hen to leave the nest, allowing inspection to commence.

Inspections should begin once the hen starts working the nest—a good indication of this is a dirty water bowl. Rosella hens bathe regularly when working the nest to carry as much moisture as possible into the nest to generate extra humidity. The nest should be inspected daily until the hen commences sitting. If everything appears normal, the hen may be left alone until she has been sitting for approximately 10 days—then the fertility of the eggs can be examined.

European aviculturists use these nest bases to prevent damage to the eggs if the hen rolls them in the nest

If the eggs are fertile—to avoid disturbing the hen—I inspect the nest once more before the eggs are due to hatch—unless the hen is off the nest. Once the chicks have hatched, inspections must take place every 2–3 days until the hen starts to leave the nest on her own.

If the entire clutch is infertile then the eggs should be discarded and the hen enticed to lay a second clutch. If only a couple of the eggs are fertile, then eggs from another pair may be fostered under the hen, or her eggs could be fostered out to another hen. Discard all cracked or rotten eggs.

A regular inspection program may allow an aviculturist to rectify unusual problems in the nest. Eastern Rosella hens in particular have a habit of continually turning over the nest material after incubation has started. Other hens may start to incubate the eggs and sit on them for a couple of weeks before deciding to smash them all, turn the nest material over and start again. Some European breeders place a tray constructed from plastic or timber in the bottom of the nest that prevents the hen from rolling the eggs around in the nest. These are available commercially throughout Europe—I am surprised that Australian breeders have not incorporated this great idea.

Most rosella species generally lay large clutches of eggs—some more than six—often the last 2–3 chicks in the nest fall behind the older siblings in their development. These chicks should be monitored during regular inspections and either fostered to other hens or removed for handraising.

If chicks die for no apparent reason, steps should be taken to rectify the problem or to remove the remaining chicks before all are lost.

Fledging

The fledging period for young rosellas is a critical time. Severe injuries or death can occur within minutes of the fledglings leaving the confines of the nest.

There are a number of steps that may minimise damage to fledglings. Excessively long flights should be avoided as they allow the young to generate too much speed before hitting the wire or the aviary frame. Hessian bags may be hung at both ends of the inside of the aviary to soften the impact and provide something for the birds to cling to as they become orientated. Branches of gum, bottlebrush or other native plants can be placed around the aviary to slow the flight—making it harder for the young to generate speed and to provide security.

Fledging of a Wild Eastern Rosella

Over the past 10 plus years—since moving to the Hunter Valley—I have placed many nesting logs and nestboxes around my property to provide wild Eastern Rosellas with somewhere to nest.

Soon after moving to the area I observed a pair of Golden-mantled Rosellas inspecting a large Elk Horn *Platycerium bifurcatum* under an awning off my garage where we were living at the time. The following day I hung a hollow log—previously used by Blue-cheeked Rosellas—adjacent to the Elk Horn. After approximately one week, the hen had started working the log in preparation for nesting. The log was situated only 3 metres from a sliding glass door and I was able to sit inside and watch this pair of rosellas going about their breeding tasks.

This pair raised six chicks and fledging was quite an experience to witness. During the early days of fledging, the first of the young was called to the top of the log by the parents—who were sitting on a clothes line approximately 15 metres from the nest. The chick travelled in a south-westerly direction from the west-facing nest, not far above the ground—perhaps a maximum of 20 metres—straight over the parents on the clothes line.

The parents flew to the chick and the cock began continually 'bumping' from the right-hand side eventually turning the chick so it was travelling in a north-easterly direction into a gully of eucalypt trees. This whole exercise took approximately one minute and was a great sight to experience.

After presumably securing their first fledging in a safe tree for the night, the parents came back later in the afternoon to care for their remaining chicks. We witnessed four of the six chicks fledged from that nest and they all fledged in the same manner, with the cock 'bumping' them along the way in the same direction.

Three other pairs of Eastern Rosellas have used the same nest site since that original pair, but nothing has quite beaten that first fledging!

Fostering

Fostering is used by aviculturists worldwide. It involves moving eggs or chicks from one hen species to another. Generally, fostering will maximise the number of chicks reared of a particular species or mutation.

The developing nest of wild Eastern Rosellas

Chicks of any of the rosella species can be reared by each other—even species such as the Red-rumped Parrot and the New Zealand Kakariki make suitable foster parents for rosella chicks. Although I am unaware of any recorded cases of fostering under species such as the Mallee Ringnecked Parrot and Port Lincoln Parrot, they should be capable of successfully rearing rosella chicks.

Steve Slade attempted to foster Eastern Rosella chicks under a pair of Princess Parrots. Unfortunately this was unsuccessful as the birds would not feed the chicks—perhaps because rosellas do not make the same food begging sound as a Princess Parrot chick. However, another breeder has achieved success fostering Princess Parrot chicks under Eastern Rosellas.

When fostering mutation progeny, all chicks must be able to be identified in the nest—particularly when dealing with normal-coloured birds split for a particular mutation. Some aviculturists wait until the chicks are old enough to place leg rings on prior to fostering under other birds. Food colouring can be also used to identify chicks when they are young. This dye is available in a variety of colours and can be purchased from most supermarkets. It is not harmful to the chicks—however chicks should not be moved until the dye is dry otherwise they may all become coated with the same colouring.

Leg Rings

Leg rings or leg bands are a popular method of identifying mutations and Normal birds—identifying unrelated young birds and reducing the chance of pairing or selling related birds.

Closed rings are preferable to split rings as a split ring may become crushed—resulting in a leg injury to the bird or the loss of a leg.

Rings should be placed when the chicks are approximately 8–10 days of age and examined a day or two later to ensure they have not fallen off and that the rear toes have not become stuck inside the ring.

The main disadvantage of leg rings are that they may become caught on items such as a small piece of wire, a twig, a small gap in the aviary cladding or behind a nestbox. I once kept an Eastern Rosella hen that caught her leg ring on the aviary door closing spring.

Following is a table of recommended minimum leg ring sizes for all rosella species. Where there are two sizes indicated, I recommend using the smallest ring possible to minimise the chance of the ring becoming caught.

Leg Ring Sizes

ROSELLA SPECIES	RING MEASUREMENT IN MILLIMETRES	RING NUMBER SIZE
Western	4.6	8
Eastern	5.6–6.1	9–10
Northern	5.6–6.1	9–10
Blue-cheeked	5.6–6.1	9–10
Pale-headed	6.1	10
Crimson	6.1–7.35	10–11
Adelaide	6.1–7.35	10–11
Yellow	7.35	11
Green	7.35	11

Record Keeping

It is imperative that accurate records of all birds bred and accommodated be kept by all aviculturists. An accurate and easily maintained record keeping system is particularly valuable to breeders of rosella mutations.

Record when eggs are laid and when incubation has commenced—this will provide you with an informed idea as to when to examine the fertility of the eggs and assist you to calculate the hatch date.

Some aviculturists record young bred from various pairs that are discarded once the young have been sold. However, others keep extensive records of everything related to their breeding programs—the dates and number of eggs laid and hatched, the number of chicks reared by individual hens and pairs, ring numbers and details of their sale.

A range of computer software designed specifically for parrot breeding programs are available, or you may prefer to keep handwritten records using the following template.

European Lutino Eastern Rosella. It is vital to keep accurate records when breeding mutations

Breeding Record Template

CAGE NUMBER		SPECIES	
COCK		**HEN**	
Type		Type	
Ring Number		Ring Number	
First Egg		First Egg	
Set Date		Set Date	
Total Eggs		Total Eggs	
Hatch Date		Hatch Date	
Number Hatched		Number Hatched	
Fledge Date		Fledge Date	
Number Fledged		Number Fledged	
Notes			

Hybridisation

Hybridisation may be used to re-establish a near extinct species, however there is no need to hybridise any of the rosella species needlessly—I discourage such a practice.

The development of mutations through the hybridisation of two species—or 'transmutation' as it is named in Europe—has been practised for many years in Australia and Europe. Breeders should be vigilant when investing in rosella mutations developed through hybridisation. All of the rosella species will produce fertile hybrids with each other and can produce offspring when mated with the Mallee Ringnecked, Port Lincoln, Twenty-eight, Red-rumped, Blue-bonnet, Mulga, Superb and Red-capped Parrots—although the vast majority are infertile.

Many years ago, Mal Stevenson, of Singleton, New South Wales, bred an Eastern Rosella hybrid Red-rumped Parrot with a Mallee Ringnecked Parrot that produced fertile eggs and went on to successfully rear the chicks—this is extremely rare. Stan Sindel and Jim Gill (1999) recorded two other hybrids with the Eastern Rosella—a Galah and a Cockatiel.

When discussing mutations in the species chapters, I do not differentiate between the development of colours from pure species and hybridisation as I believe it would be impossible to be correct in all cases.

Inbreeding

Inbreeding relates to the mating of two closely related birds—such as brother and sister, father and daughter or mother and son. This breeding method should be discouraged as it can lead to genetic defects such as infertility and unusually small young.

Mutation breeders may be forced to revert to inbreeding to establish a particular mutation, particularly a recessive mating. This should then be followed by outcrossing—unrelated breeding—commonly practised in order to establish and maintain a strong mutant strain.

Handrearing

The following section is a brief overview of handrearing. For more in-depth information—necessary when handrearing any parrot species—consult the specialist title ***A Guide to Incubation and Handrearing Parrots*** published and available through ***ABK Publications***.

At some stage during breeding it may become necessary to remove chicks for handrearing. Whether this is done by choice or to save a chick's life, it is recommended to always have handrearing mix available.

There are a variety of adequate commercial handrearing diets in Australia. My preference is a homemade mix consisting of sunflower kernels, human baby cereal, chicken starter crumbles, breadcrumbs and raw peanuts. The ingredients are mixed together and ground to a fine powder in a food processor. I seldom encounter crop-related problems in chicks reared on this mix—they also achieve excellent growth rates.

Rosellas are relatively simple to handrear. They can be removed from the nest at 10 days of age and before their eyes have opened. A brooder or small plastic bin incorporating a heat source such as a heat pad will be required. The heat source may be removed gradually when birds begin to feather. To allow for acclimatisation, it should be turned off during the day and switched on at night for a few days.

A cup warmer maintains the temperature of the handrearing mix

Depending on the size and age of the bird, it will generally require 4–6 feeds per day, provided at regular intervals between 6am and 10pm. As a chick grows the crop holds more food—the number of feeds and time between feeds is gradually reduced over time.

Food should be heated to a temperature of approximately 40°C. A young chick will throw its head around if food is too hot and refuse to eat if food is too cold. A great asset to the handrearer is a cup or mug warmer—to maintain the temperature of the handrearing mix.

Newcomers to handrearing should use a bent spoon to feed the chicks. This may be a slower method of feeding than using a syringe or crop tube but it will avoid potential problems such as burnt crops from the food being too hot and candida and fungus-related problems due to bacteria residing in the syringes and tubes. All handrearing utensils should be sterilised in an antibacterial solution.

Young handreared rosellas will fledge earlier than parent-reared, therefore the chicks should be moved into small, all-wire cages as soon as they begin to attempt to climb out of their brooding box. Chicks can become quite flighty at this stage therefore an enclosed area is advisable to prevent injuries.

When chicks are placed into a cage they should be supplied with dry seeds and softfoods—canary seed, panicum, French White and Japanese millets and greenfood such as endive, chicory and lettuce are ideal. Although the chicks will often wean themselves, handrearing mix should still be offered—but it should not be forced upon the chicks. As long as they are eating they will continue to grow into healthy birds.

The following tables compare the average and maximum weight gains taken from a selection of 30 specimens of various rosella species handreared and recorded over a 15 year period. They were fed a variety of commercial handrearing mixes including Lakes™, Roudybush™ and my own homemade recipe.

GROWTH CHARTS

EASTERN ROSELLA

DAYS	AVERAGE WEIGHT in grams	HIGHEST WEIGHT in grams	DAYS	AVERAGE WEIGHT in grams	HIGHEST WEIGHT in grams
1			19	81	90
2			20	85	94
3			21	88	98
4	17.3	30	22	89	98
5	21.3	32	23	92	104
6	21.3	36	24	92	104
7	28	38	25	95	106
8	30	40	26	98	108
9	35.5	40	27	100	108
10	38.5	44	28	102	110
11	48	58	29	102.5	110
12	50.5	60	30	103	112
13	56	68	31	103	114
14	63	74	32	102.5	110
15	67.5	80	33	102.7	106
16	72.5	86	34	103.3	106
17	75.5	86	35	104	108
18	79	88			

BLUE-CHEEKED ROSELLA

DAYS	AVERAGE WEIGHT in grams	HIGHEST WEIGHT in grams
1		
2		
3		
4		
5		
6		
7		
8	50	52
9	51.2	54
10	52.7	56
11	54	58
12	56.5	62
13	58	64
14	62.5	74
15	65.5	70
16	72	74
17	76.7	78
18	82	82
19	83.3	84
20	84	86
21	88.5	90
22	88.8	92
23	90.4	92
24	93.2	98
25	95.6	96
26	97.6	98
27	100	100
28	100	102
29	101.5	104
30	102	102
31	102.5	104
32	102	104
33	102.5	104
34	101	106
35	101	102

PALE-HEADED ROSELLA

DAYS	AVERAGE WEIGHT in grams	HIGHEST WEIGHT in grams
1		
2		
3		
4	22.5	26
5	25.5	30
6	29	34
7	33	40
8	37.5	46
9	42	52
10	47	58
11	49.5	60
12	51	60
13	54	64
14	56.5	66
15	58	68
16	59	68
17	60	68
18	63	70
19	67	76
20	70	82
21	73.5	84
22	80	92
23	85	94
24	89.5	98
25	91.5	98
26	93.5	98
27	96.5	98
28	99.5	100
29	100.5	102
30	104	106
31	107.5	110
32	108.5	112
33	111.5	116
34	113.5	120
35	115	124

NORTHERN ROSELLA

DAYS	AVERAGE WEIGHT in grams	HIGHEST WEIGHT in grams	DAYS	AVERAGE WEIGHT in grams	HIGHEST WEIGHT in grams
1			19	63.7	78
2			20	67	84
3			21	73	86
4			22	75	90
5	8.7	18	23	77	90
6	14	22	24	80.7	92
7	17	28	25	83	92
8	18.5	32	26	85.3	94
9	21.2	34	27	86	94
10	24.3	34	28	87	94
11	27.3	36	29	90	92
12	29.7	40	30	91.3	92
13	33	44	31	92	92
14	37.3	52	32	92	94
15	41.7	56	33	92	92
16	46.7	62	34	89	94
17	51.7	68	35	90	94
18	58	74			

WESTERN ROSELLA

DAYS	AVERAGE WEIGHT in grams	HIGHEST WEIGHT in grams	DAYS	AVERAGE WEIGHT in grams	HIGHEST WEIGHT in grams
1			19	40	48
2			20	42.5	50
3			21	47.5	52
4			22	49	54
5			23	51.5	62
6			24	56	58
7	13	16	25	59.5	64
8	16	20	26	58	60
9	19	24	27	60	62
10	22	28	28	59.5	62
11	25	32	29	61.5	64
12	28	36	30	61.5	64
13	31	40	31	63	64
14	35	42	32		
15	37.5	44	33		
16	35	44	34		
17	38	40	35		
18	38	42			

Crimson Rosella

HEALTH AND DISEASES

Disclaimer

This chapter is designed to assist bird owners to understand disease in their birds. It is not meant or designed to take the place of the person best qualified to assist you in the diagnosis and treatment of your bird—your avian veterinarian. Nor is it, by any means, a complete A–Z of rosella diseases—it would take an entire book to cover all of these, not just a chapter. It cannot be stressed enough—if you have a sick bird, take it to an avian veterinarian. Pet shop and folklore remedies rarely work, and the time wasted while waiting for a response can be the difference between a live bird and a dead one.

Any treatments or procedures described in this book are meant to help you understand bird health better. The author and publisher accept no responsibility or liability for any person using these treatments without direct veterinary advice.

General Information

Rosellas, as comparatively small to medium birds, can be found fairly close to the bottom of the food chain, despite their sometimes aggressive nature. In common with many other 'prey' species, evolutionary instincts have taught them that predators (eg falcons, snakes and quolls) prefer to single out the bird that looks slightly different—particularly if it looks sick and easy to catch. Therefore, one of a bird's survival instincts is to *not* look sick.

One hundred years of domestication cannot cancel out millions of years of evolution. Our pet and aviary rosellas still retain the instinct to hide signs of illness until they are very sick. To us, as aviculturists, this means that often the first signs of illness are seen at the end of the illness—not the beginning. The natural reaction to 'wait and see' can therefore be a death sentence for many sick birds.

You also need to be aware that sick rosellas will often all show the same signs of disease—regardless of the cause. Nearly all sick birds will fluff their feathers, sit still and close their eyes. This is a response to disease, which is designed to conserve energy and body heat. It is not characteristic of any one disease—it simply means that the bird is sick.

As a bird owner you need to be alert for early signs of illness. Once seen and recognised, you then have to act on them quickly. The sooner a bird receives treatment, the better its chances of survival. A veterinarian cannot tell you what is wrong with your bird over the phone. The longer it takes for the bird to be physically examined, the higher the chances of severe illness or death, and the higher the cost of treatment will be.

Golden-mantled Eastern Rosellas showing signs of illness.

Recognising a Sick Bird

Remember—birds are masters of deception. They are able to hide any signs of illness to avoid attracting the attention of a predator. Birds will only look sick when they are so sick that they cannot hide it anymore. However, there are subtle signs that an alert owner can detect. The following behaviours are not normal—

- A bird that is usually very vocal and active—chattering and calling, and flying or climbing around a cage all day long—but then sits quietly in a corner of the cage.
- A bird that is fluffed up. It may appear normal when you approach, but will then fluff up again a few minutes later.
- A bird that normally comes down and starts eating as soon as food is placed in the dish, but is now not interested in food.
- A bird that eats continuously and ravenously.
- A bird that sits on the floor of the cage.
- A bird that starts to drink water excessively, or not at all.
- A bird that drinks a lot of water and then vomits or regurgitates.
- A bird that sleeps a lot, particularly with both feet on the perch.
- A bird that starts sneezing a lot, or has a discharge from its nostrils, or rubs its eyes on the perch or with its foot.
- An excessive amount of water in a bird's droppings, unless that bird is a lorikeet.
- A bird that has diarrhoea—the urates (the white part of the droppings) are green.
- Bleeding from anywhere.
- The appearance of bald patches or abnormal feathers.

This bird's eyelids are drooping—if this persists for more than a few minutes, it is strongly suggestive that the bird is unwell and a veterinary examination warranted

If you see these signs, *now* is the time to act. Waiting a few days 'to see if the bird gets better' is often a death sentence for a bird struggling to recover its health.

Keeping Your Birds Healthy

It is not difficult to appreciate that, given the increasing costs of veterinary care and medications, it makes much more sense to prevent disease rather than treat it. There are a few things that aviculturists can do to ensure that their birds stay healthy—

- Prevent disease from entering your collection through quarantine measures.
- Have a plan and a set of procedures in place to minimise the spread of disease within a collection if disease is somehow introduced.
- Minimise the stress on the birds by carefully managing them. This can be achieved, for example, by providing appropriate aviary design, minimising the birds' access to people within the aviary complex and ensuring that the birds are not 'pushed too hard' to maximise production.
- Feed a healthy diet suitable for the species, the age and according to breeding periods.
- Have a preventative treatment plan in place to minimise the impact of parasites.
- Remain constantly alert to detect sick birds and take appropriate action when necessary.

Quarantine Procedures

Quarantine serves two purposes. Firstly, it minimises the risks of introducing disease and parasites into a collection. Secondly, it gives a new bird the chance to become acclimatised to a new management and dietary regimen before having to deal with the stress of establishing a social pecking order in its new home. Both of these purposes are equally important but are often overlooked by inexperienced aviculturists in their haste to see a new bird out in an aviary.

Quarantine cages can be as complex as a separate flight or as simple as a large cage. Whatever you use, it must be geographically isolated from other birds in the collection. Placing a new bird into a spare flight in a bank of aviaries does ***not*** constitute quarantine.

Birds in quarantine cages must be managed in exactly the same way as your other birds—the same kind of feed dishes, feeding times and diet—but must be fed and watered *last*. No matter how keen you are each morning to see your new purchase, it must be the last bird attended to. This simple step prevents you backtracking to your existing collection, perhaps with contaminated faecal material on shoes, clothing or hands.

Feed and water dishes, catching nets and any other equipment you use must not be taken from the quarantine area to the rest of the collection, and vice versa.

The quarantine period also provides a good opportunity to treat your bird for parasites. Spraying the bird with a good quality lice spray every two weeks for three treatments will prevent external parasites being introduced into your collection. Worming—preferably with a crop needle—should be done at least twice and its efficacy then evaluated by a faecal test by your local veterinarian. Any veterinarian can perform this simple test—you do not have to live near an avian veterinarian to get this done. This last step is very important. Not all worm medications are effective, and you should never assume any particular medication has worked.

Disease testing can also be done at this stage. At a minimum, birds should be tested for Psittacine Beak and Feather Disease virus (PBFD) and Psittacosis. You might also want to consider screening for Polyomavirus and Megabacteria. Discuss this with your local avian veterinarian, but a word of warning: failure to do this may well cost you dearly. The introduction of disease into an aviary is a major cause of production loss in aviculture.

The recommended quarantine period is six weeks. In this time you need to watch your bird closely for any signs of disease. (See *Recognising the Sick Bird* on page 70.) If you introduce any new birds into quarantine at this time, they should be placed in their own quarantine cage in a separate location. If this is not feasible, the new arrivals must be placed in the same cage as the previously quarantined bird. You must therefore re-start your quarantine clock, ie the six week period starts from the time the new birds arrive.

Performed carefully, thoroughly and with some forethought, quarantine can be the simplest and cheapest form of disease control that aviculturists can use.

Minimising the Spread of Disease

Despite the best quarantine procedures, disease can still be introduced into an aviary. If plans and procedures to minimise its spread are not already in place, this disease can 'explode' within an aviary complex, resulting in the loss of many valuable birds and/or an expensive lesson to the bird keeper.

First and foremost, bird keepers must be alert to the presence of a sick bird and have a contingency plan in place for what to do when a sick bird is detected. A 'wait and see' approach is often regretted by aviculturists confronted with a contagious disease.

A hospital cage should be readily available, and not be something that has to be improvised at the time of need. (Note—the hospital area is NOT the same as the quarantine area.) Veterinary advice should be sought as soon as possible—unless you know what you are dealing with, it is impossible to take appropriate precautions.

However, before disease breaks out, it is important to manage the collection as if a disease were already present. Divide your collection into areas, based on vulnerability to disease and/or importance to you—the nursery, juvenile holding cages, breeding aviaries and quarantine.

- Geographically separate these areas, making it less likely that airborne transmission of disease will occur.
- Keep catching nets, feed and water dishes and other equipment in each of these areas separate from those in other areas—do not 'mix and match'. If you do, one day you will slip up in your cleaning—and regret it!
- Birds in the most vulnerable and the most important areas should be fed first, moving to the other areas in descending order of vulnerability and importance. For example, carrying disease from some pet pigeons housed closer to your feeding station, or to a valuable collection of parrot colour mutations, simply does not make sense.

By assuming and planning for the worst you can prevent, or at least minimise, the spread of an introduced disease. It may seem like a lot of work but you need to think of it as an insurance policy. Most of us have our cars, houses, and health insured—but do we really want to collect on those policies? Putting the effort into implementing the above concepts will hopefully mean you will never need to collect on this insurance policy!

Better Health Through Effective Management

How an aviary is managed will have a major impact on the incidence of infections. No matter what you do, it is inevitable that your birds will be exposed to infectious agents. How the birds are managed, however, will often determine the likelihood of infectious disease occurring, whether and how it will spread throughout the aviary, and what effect it will have on your birds.

Housing density, selection of high quality stock, the use of quarantine flights, the level of hygiene maintained within an aviary, the use (and misuse) of medications, parasite control, insect and other pest control, and the degree of veterinary involvement in aviary management are just some of the key management factors that will have an effect on the incidence of disease within an aviary.

Nutrition is also a major management factor in disease prevention. As incredible as it sounds, there are still many aviculturists who consider seed to be a complete and 'natural' diet for birds. Nothing could be further from the truth! Seed diets are deficient in vitamins, minerals, and protein and have excessive levels of fat and carbohydrates. Seed can be a small part of a healthy diet, but it is by no means a complete diet. A poor diet affects the resistance of your birds to an introduced disease and losses will almost certainly be higher than they would be if your birds were on a healthy diet. See *Malnutrition* on page 77.

The normal stresses that a bird is subjected to in its lifetime, such as temperature extremes, weaning, breeding, rearing young, showing and sales will impose a certain degree of immunosuppression on an individual bird or flock. In normal conditions this stress is to be expected and the bird(s) should cope without any difficulty. However, when combined with other stressors such as overcrowding or poor hygiene, they can become major contributing factors to the susceptibility of an individual or flock to disease.

Another factor predisposing birds to disease is the immunosuppression caused by the presence of concurrent diseases. Multiple bacterial, fungal, viral and parasitic infections are often diagnosed in sick birds. A responsible aviculturist will look past the obvious problem and examine the bird and flock for the presence of other diseases that may be having an indirect effect on the disease status of the bird(s).

Checklist for Factors Predisposing Birds to Disease

Aviary Design	• Housing density. Overcrowded flights are infinitely more susceptible to stress and disease. • Ventilation. Poorly ventilated flights lead to 'foul air'—caused by increased levels of ammonia and dust—which promotes the rapid spread of airborne diseases. • Climate control. Lack of shade, or an excess of shade can lead to stress, poor hygiene and disease. • Drainage. Damp aviaries will obviously be a breeding ground for disease. • Ease of cleaning: – wooden frames versus metal frames – floor, ie dirt, sand, concrete or wire – flight furniture, ie perches, dishes, nestboxes.
General Management	• Stock selection. Buying 'cheap' birds almost always ends in disaster. Buy the best birds you can afford, even if it means bypassing a 'bargain'. • 'Life stage' management. The nursery should be managed differently to the juvenile flights, and the juvenile flights differently to the breeder flights. • Hygiene. Regular cleaning of the flights and flight furniture and replacement of nesting material and perches will reduce the buildup of pathogens and therefore minimise the risk of disease. • Biosecurity. See *Quarantine* on page 71 and *Minimising the Spread of Disease* on page 71. • Medication Program. Drugs are not a substitute for good management. Be very wary of advice to use drugs in your aviary on a frequent basis. The strategic use of anti-parasitic drugs and/or antibiotics, however, can be a useful tool in some (not all) collections. Such use needs to be worked out in consultation with an avian veterinarian who knows your collection. • Insect and pest control. Cockroaches, biting insects, rats and mice can all spread disease. An ongoing and systematic control and eradication program must be in place. • Veterinary involvement. Trying to keep large numbers of birds without any veterinary costs, while it may sound appealing, will only end up costing you a lot more in sick or dead birds. Veterinarians have been trained to recognise signs of illness, diagnose problems, treat them accordingly and then implement prevention programs—something no pet shop employee or breeder can hope to do. Remember, you get what you pay for!

Nutrition	• Appropriate diet for the age and reproductive status of the bird. • Supplements can be employed to bring the quality of a diet up—but avoid over-supplementation. • Food and water dishes – Type. Terracotta, plastic and galvanised dishes promote the growth of potential pathogens. – Number. Sufficient to ensure that all birds have equal access to food. – Location. Avoid placing dishes under the perches or in full sun.
Physiological Stress	• Climate extremes. Although birds can acclimatise to almost any weather conditions, shelter should be provided to help them avoid extreme variations in climatic conditions. • Breeding and rearing young is a stressful time for birds and this needs to be catered for in their management and nutrition. • Weaning can be very stressful for juveniles, regardless of whether they are handreared or parent reared.
Sales and Shows	• Sales and shows are obviously stressful events for birds and every effort should be made to minimise this stress. • Exposure to pathogens is increased. • Stress should be managed through caging, provision of adequate food, careful handling and the use of electrolytes in the water before, during and after the event.
Concurrent Disease	• Parasites are common in poorly managed collections. Regular control measures combined with monitoring are essential to keep an aviary's level of parasitism in check. • Bacterial, viral and fungal infections are usually the result of inadequate quarantine, poor hygiene and poor management. They are a 'symptom' of a problem in collection management, rather than a diagnosis in their own right.

COMMON DISEASES

Diseases can be broadly grouped into infectious diseases (those likely to spread from bird to bird within an aviary) and non-infectious diseases (those that are an individual problem but are unlikely to become a flock problem unless related to something such as nutrition). At times, however, there is some 'cross over' between these two groups.

Infectious Diseases

Chlamydiosis (Psittacosis)

This disease is caused by the chlamydial organism, *Chlamydophila psittaci*. Clinical signs most commonly seen include conjunctivitis (swollen eyelids, reddened conjunctiva, ocular discharge and feather loss around the eye), sinusitis (swellings around the eye, nasal discharge, staining of feathers around the nares), sneezing, diarrhoea, and green urates. However, clinical signs can be completely absent, or the bird may die suddenly without any clinical signs. Although most commonly seen in birds under stress—in new purchases, in pet shop environments or in overcrowded aviaries—Psittacosis can be seen in any bird at almost any time.

Faeces of parrots suffering from Chlamydiosis (Psittacosis)

There is a current trend amongst some aviculturists to say that 'all birds have this disease, so why worry about it?' The reasons are very simple. Firstly, this statement is simply incorrect—not all birds have this disease. This statement is usually made by people excusing their lack of preventative measures. But most importantly, ***this disease is transmissible to people.*** It causes flu-like symptoms, pneumonia and occasionally death. Seek veterinary advice immediately if your bird shows the signs of this zoonotic disease.

Gastrointestinal Infections

These infections can be due to a wide range of pathogens, including intestinal parasites, bacteria, yeast and viruses. Clinical signs can include vomiting, increased salivation, diarrhoea, whole seed in the droppings and weight loss. Death occurs due to dehydration, electrolyte loss and bacterial toxins damaging the liver and kidneys. Laboratory tests are usually required to determine the cause, and this then dictates the appropriate treatment. Affected birds must be rehydrated, usually by injections of fluids under the skin, although crop drenching with electrolytes is effective if the bird is not vomiting.

Intestinal Parasites

Internal parasites are, unfortunately, quite common in rosellas. Roundworms (ascarids) are commonly found in the intestinal tract. Their eggs can be identified under a microscope. *Coccidia*—a non-motile protozoan parasite—is also occasionally found. All of these parasites can cause weight loss, diarrhoea, and even death. Diagnosis requires faecal examination under a microscope to detect either the eggs or the parasites themselves. Treatment is determined by the type of parasite detected. As these parasites are spread through the droppings of infected birds, it is important to minimise contact between birds and their droppings. Wire floor

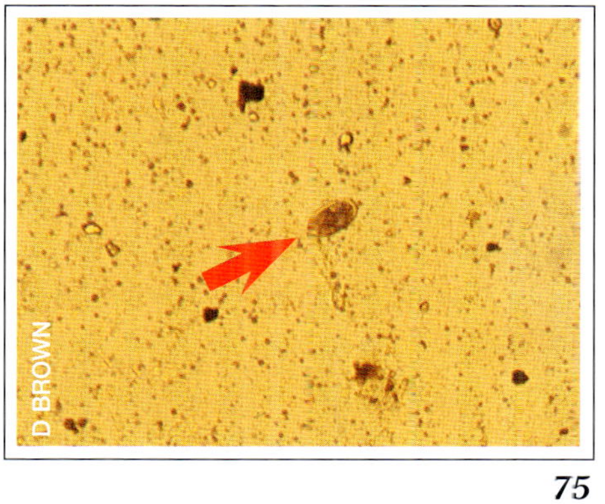

Roundworm egg as seen at 40X magnification under a microscope

cages and good hygiene are excellent methods of minimising this contact. Water and feed dishes must be located so that birds cannot defecate into them.

Megabacteria

Despite its name, Megabacteria—scientifically known as *Macrorhabdus ornithogaster*—is a fungus found in the stomach of infected birds. Birds are infected when they eat food contaminated with the droppings of another infected bird. The fungus forms a dense mat on the stomach wall, preventing digestion of the food. Ulcers may also form. The infected bird becomes ravenously hungry, but loses weight. Blood may be seen around its mouth, and diarrhoea is not uncommon. Treatment requires fluids to rehydrate the bird, an antifungal drug by mouth for 30 days, and reduction of stress. Crop feeding with an easily digested food may be necessary in some cases.

Respiratory Infections

These can occur in the sinuses, airways, lungs or air sacs. Possible causes include bacterial infections, fungal infections (Aspergillosis), *Chlamydophila psittaci* (Psittacosis), inhaled food (handrearing formula or seed) and occasionally viral infections. Parasite infections are relatively rare. Affected birds may sneeze, have discharges from the nares and eyes, swollen sinuses, open-mouth breathing and increased respiratory effort (wing droop, tail bobbing and exaggerated visible movement of the body with each breath). It must also be noted that eggbinding, enlarged internal organs and fluid in the abdomen can all put pressure on the air sacs and cause signs of respiratory distress—without actual respiratory disease being present. Veterinary attention should be sought immediately, as respiratory infections can be life threatening. The cause of the infection can rarely be determined without laboratory tests.

Psittacine Beak and Feather Disease (PBFD)

This disease, commonly seen in all rosella species, is caused by the PBFD virus, a circovirus, one of the smallest viruses known to humans. It causes the progressive replacement of normal feathers with abnormal feathers (retained sheaths and blood supply, clubbed appearance, stress lines, constrictions and abnormal shapes). Rosellas typically develop untidy plumage and lose feathers easily when handled. They often develop feather colour changes—blue or brown feathers becoming white and green feathers becoming yellow. The beak lesions that are seen in cockatoos, eg overgrown, easily fractured beaks, are rarely seen in rosellas. Immunosuppression is common, leading to death from other infections.

The virus is shed in the droppings and feather dust of infected birds. The disease may not become apparent in a newly infected bird for weeks, months or years. Diagnosis is made on clinical signs and DNA testing. Note that DNA testing should be left to an avian veterinarian to interpret, as it gives no indication as to whether a bird is infected, whether the sample is contaminated or whether the virus is just passing through the bird's body at the time of collection. There is no effective treatment, and most infected birds die within two years of secondary diseases related to immunosuppression. (Note that some birds, despite showing clinical signs, may live for many years.)

External Parasites

Lice are quite common on wild birds and in some aviaries. They feed on skin scales and feather debris—lice are not blood suckers. They live on the bird their whole life, and lay their eggs along the shaft of a feather. These eggs are easily seen with the naked eye and are known as 'nits'. The lice themselves are also usually easy to see—holding your bird's wing up to a bright light and examining the underside of it may reveal eggs and lice. Heavy infestations can make a bird itchy and give the feathers a 'moth-eaten' look.

Treatment for lice requires spraying with a pyrethrin spray or wash. Do not use sprays containing maldison or malathion. These are organophosphates and can be very poisonous both to the birds and to you. Although registered for use in birds, I know of birds that have been poisoned and died after being treated according to the manufacturer's directions. With the advent of the safer pyrethrin sprays, veterinarians no longer recommend these products. The advice given to treat pet birds every three months is inappropriate—once a pet bird has been treated properly, and so long as it is not exposed to other birds, there is generally no reason for repeated treatment.

Mites are a different proposition, as they are blood suckers. With a heavy enough burden, an infected bird may die from blood loss over a period of time. Young birds in the nest are particularly prone to this problem, as the Red Mite—the most common mite seen in aviaries—lives in the nestbox, feeding on the birds at night and leaving them by day. Therefore, examination of the nestbox during daylight hours may not reveal the presence of the mites. There are other mites that affect aviary birds, and their presence can also be difficult to detect. Some live on the bird all the time, others will leave at certain times of their life cycle or in daylight hours. Affected birds are often itchy, with damaged skin and feathers, and may be weak from blood loss. Treatment with ivermectin or moxidectin, combined with pyrethrin sprays, is usually effective. It is vital that the environment also be treated. The nestbox should be sprayed with a safe residual insecticide, eg *Coopex®*, *Cisilin®* or *Avian Insect Liquidator®*.

Non-infectious Diseases and Other Problems

Malnutrition

This is one of the greatest problems confronting rosellas in captivity. An all-seed and, conversely, an all-pellet diet are causing more problems with health and longevity than infectious diseases and poor husbandry combined. It is a myth that rosellas are wholly seed-eaters. In the wild they consume a wide range of foods. Ripened agricultural grain is only a relative newcomer to their diet. Seed is high in fat and carbohydrates, and low in virtually everything else, eg protein, vitamins and minerals. Birds fed this sort of diet develop the same problems that people eating high-fat diets do, including obesity, liver disease, diabetes and cardiovascular disease. On the other hand, all-pellet diets may lead to kidney disease. A balance must be struck by feeding a mixture of seeds, sprouted seed, fruits, leafy green vegetables and pellets. (See *Feeding* on page 41). Your avian veterinarian will be able to advise you on a healthy diet for your rosella.

Trauma

This is unfortunately quite common in the pugnacious rosella. Scalping, beak injuries, wingtip trauma and even broken limbs are all seen with this species. Immediate first aid (see page 78) should be given and the bird transported to an avian veterinarian for a more thorough assessment and treatment.

Kidney Disease

This can be due to a wide range of conditions—zinc and lead poisoning, bacterial infections and an all-pellet diet, to name just a few. It is characterised by increased thirst and very watery droppings. If recognised early and treated aggressively, kidney disease can be reversed in many cases. Long-term kidney disease can lead to the development of gout—the deposition of uric acid into the joints—causing painful swellings of the joints and lameness. This condition is extremely difficult to treat, as only temporary pain relief is usually possible.

The sloppiness of this dropping is due to excess urates not the faeces. This is called polyuria, not diarrhoea, and is a sign of kidney disease

Liver Disease

Liver disease is due to a wide range of conditions. In rosellas the two most common problems are Psittacosis and obesity (fatty liver). In acute cases, affected birds often present with green urates, excessive urine in their droppings and non-specific signs of illness. Longer-term cases often have darkened or greasy-looking feathers, an overgrown beak and weight loss. Fortunately the liver is a resilient organ. Once the problem is recognised and the cause identified, appropriate treatment usually results in complete recovery.

Zinc and Lead Poisoning

Metal poisoning is still far too common. Both lead and zinc can be acute poisons, but lead can also be a cumulative toxin, ie a small amount taken into the body is stored, and when the levels are high enough, poisoning results. Both poisons will cause increased thirst, vomiting and watery droppings. Lead is also more likely to cause neurological signs such as fits and convulsions, paralysis and sometimes foot-chewing. Once again, prompt recognition and appropriate treatment are usually successful.

Reproductive Disease

This is a common consequence of the reproductive prowess of the rosella. When combined with an inadequate diet (usually seed without any supplementation) and a lack of exercise, the rosella's ability to start egg laying at an early age and then keep on laying egg after egg is a recipe for disaster. Eggbinding, uterine infections, yolk peritonitis and cloacal prolapses are all common. These conditions are frequently fatal in rosellas if not treated aggressively. For more advice, you should consult your avian veterinarian.

First Aid for the Sick Bird

First aid for birds is, like first aid for people, *not* a substitute for veterinary care. However, first aid *can* be the difference between life and death for a sick or injured bird. All bird owners need to be familiar with the basics of first aid and be prepared to implement them if necessary.

A sick bird has three main requirements—warmth, fluids and food.

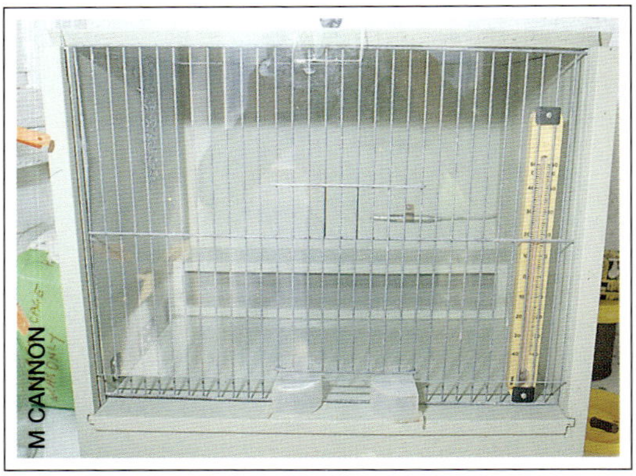

A suitable hospital cage. Place a heat source next to this cage to provide warmth

A bird's normal body temperature is 41°C. This is reached by absorbing heat from the surrounding air (the ambient temperature), and then generating the balance by metabolising food to produce energy (and therefore heat). When a sick bird is not eating much its production of metabolic energy is decreased. Its body temperature starts to drop, so it fluffs its feathers to trap body heat. If its temperature continues to drop, it will become hypothermic, go into shock and die. This will usually happen before the bird dies of whatever has made it sick in the first place.

Therefore sick birds need to be warmed up—urgently. Placing a blanket over its cage will not help—the bird is not generating enough heat for the blanket to trap and keep warm. The most effective way to warm a bird up is to place it under a light—a bulb, not a fluoro. The heat generated by the bulb will raise the ambient temperature to 35–40°C quickly, making the bird much more comfortable. The bulb should be located close to the cage, right beside or above a perch. This allows the bird to get right up to it if it wants, and to move away if it feels too hot. The light needs to be left on 24 hours a day, until the bird is no longer seeking its warmth. By warming the bird up, you overcome hypothermic shock and allow the bird to direct its metabolism towards getting better, rather than just keeping warm. Try not to disturb or handle the bird too much until it becomes more active. You need to remain patient until it is feeling stronger.

Warming a bird up is the single most important thing that you can do for it. Do not try to do anything else for an hour or so, until the bird is becoming more alert and active. Once you have it under a light, contact your veterinarian to make an appointment—do not ask your veterinarian for a diagnosis or treatment over the phone—it just cannot be done. All sick birds look the same—it is only by getting a thorough history, doing a careful physical examination and using appropriate laboratory tests that your veterinarian can determine the problem and suggest an appropriate treatment. Anything else is just a guess, and it is unfair to place your veterinarian in such a situation.

If you cannot get to the veterinarian immediately, the next thing to do is to get some fluids into your bird. If it is drinking well (and not vomiting), adding some glucose powder to the water may be all that you need to do. Place one teaspoon of the powder into 100ml of water and let the bird drink as much as it likes. If the bird is not drinking at all, or is not drinking enough, you need to give it the fluids, either with an eye-dropper or a crop needle. If you are comfortable injecting fluids, administering 5% of the bird's body weight, twice daily, under the skin is quite effective.

Offer your bird a variety of foods. If it is not eating, you may need to crop feed it with a handrearing formula. If you don't have this handy, a vegetable/fruit baby food will be adequate in the short term.

Do not give fluids or food to your bird until it has warmed up. A weak bird given fluids or food by mouth could easily choke on them.

Basic First Aid for the Injured Bird

The basic requirements for an injured bird are similar to those of a sick bird. The bird needs to be kept warm, take in fluids and eat, if it is to survive. However, trauma has its own problems, including bleeding, the risk of further injury and breathing difficulties. Try not to do too much too soon or too quickly. It is better to do one thing quickly, put the bird down for a while, and then pick it up and do something else. Trying to do everything at once can stress the bird to an extreme.

If the bird shows signs of bleeding, determine if it is still bleeding and where it is bleeding from. A small amount of blood can look like a lot spread over a bird's feathers and give the impression that it is bleeding to death.

If the bird is bleeding from a broken 'blood' feather—a newly erupted feather with blood in the shaft—try pinching the feather between your thumb and forefinger for 30–60 seconds. In most cases this will stop the bleeding—if it continues, pluck the feather out and pinch off the feather follicle to stop any bleeding. A bleeding toenail can be treated by pushing the nail into a wet bar of soap. The soap will form a plug over the nail and stop the bleeding. Dry Condy's crystals (potassium permanganate) will do the same.

If the bleeding is coming from anywhere else, or you cannot get it to stop, seek veterinary assistance urgently. If possible, maintain finger pressure until you get to the veterinarian.

A broken wing or leg, left unsplinted, can get swung around, stepped on, bitten, and generally injured more than the original break. Sometimes this subsequent damage is so bad that the limb has to be amputated. Taping the wing to the body with sticky tape, or strapping a broken leg, can prevent further damage. It also markedly reduces the amount of pain and stress that your bird is feeling.

If your bird is having difficulty breathing—opening its mouth, heaving its body up and down, tail bobbing, or making audible wheezes, grunts or rattles with each breath—go straight to the veterinarian. Emergency treatment can save many of these birds, but not if they are left for a day or two.

Things *Not* to Do

- Do not give your bird alcohol or coffee as 'a stimulant'.
- Do not give your bird old antibiotics or pet shop remedies. These rarely work and waste time while waiting for a recovery response.
- Do not ring your neighbour, your uncle or another breeder for advice. Just go to see your veterinarian as soon as possible. First aid is not a substitute for veterinary care.
- Do not assume that you know what is wrong with your bird.

Supply of Prescription Medications

Virtually every country in the world has a Health Department which, amongst other things, regulates the supply of prescription drugs (eg antibiotics, pain killers and sedatives) to both people and animals. These regulations make it very clear to veterinarians that the supply of these medications for the treatment of animals not under their direct care is illegal. 'Direct Care' means that the veterinarian must have recently examined and diagnosed the animal in question for the disease problem for which the medication is required. Put simply, this means that unless the veterinarian has seen your birds, for this disease, within the last few months, it is illegal for that veterinarian to dispense any prescription medications such as antibiotics.

These regulations exist to protect both you and your birds. The indiscriminate use of drugs will eventually mean that many of these drugs will become useless. Then, when either you or your birds need that drug in an emergency, it may not work.

Asking your veterinarian to supply you with antibiotics or other drugs for birds that he/she has not seen is asking your veterinarian to break the law and risk heavy fines and/or deregistration. Unless you are willing to guarantee payment of these fines and financially support your veterinarian while he/she is deregistered (and therefore unable to practise as a veterinarian), please do not ask your veterinarian to break the law in order to save yourself a consultation fee and some laboratory tests.

Crimson Rosella

SPECIES

Adelaide Rosella

P ODEKERKEN

P ODEKERKEN

Eastern Rosella cock

EASTERN ROSELLA
Platycercus eximius

Other Names
Golden-mantled Rosella (a common name for the *P. e. elecica* subspecies), White-cheeked Rosella, Common Rosella, Red Rosella, Red-headed Rosella, Yellow-mantled Rosella, Splendid Rosella
German: Rosellasittich
Dutch: Prachtrosella
French: Perruche omnicolore

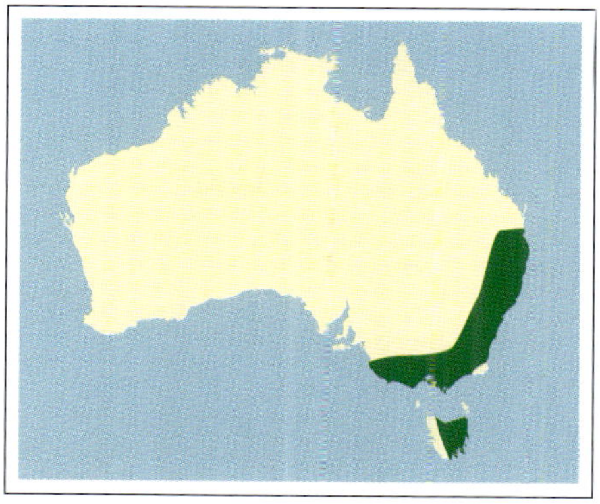

DESCRIPTION

Adult
Length: 30cm
Weight: 110 grams
Iris: Brown
Legs: Grey
Beak: Grey

A very popular bird, the Eastern Rosella is commonly recognised for its bright colouration and swift flight. It is usually seen in small groups or family parties in the wild and can be observed throughout towns and cities within its range.

Cock
The head, nape and upper chest are bright red and the cheekpatches are white. The mantle feathers are black with green-yellow edging. The lower chest is yellow, merging to green on the abdomen. The uppertail coverts and rump are also green. The scapulars are black and the shoulder-patches are dark blue. The tail feathers are green with blue edging and the vent is red.

Hen
The hen displays slight sexual dimorphism and is slightly smaller than the cock. The upper mandible is narrower and the overall colouration is duller. The yellow scalloping on the mantle is paler than that of the cock and the lower chest is more green than yellow.

Juvenile
Juveniles are a duller version of the adult hen. The head and chest of the juvenile cock is often brighter red and the upper mandible is slightly wider and thicker than that of a young hen. Juvenile hens display green around the nape and hind-neck, rather than red, and the scalloping of the mantle is less defined. The underwing stripe is visible.

Eastern Rosella hen

Subspecies and Racial Variations

The Eastern Rosella was first described as *Psittacus eximius* by Shaw and Nodder in 1792. It was reclassified as *Platycercus eximius* by Vigors in 1825.

The Golden-mantled Rosella subspecies was first described by John Gould as *P. e. splendidus* in 1845 and later named *P. e. cecilae* by Gregory Mathews in 1912. In 1989 Schodde and Short proposed the name be changed to *P. e. elecica*—the current taxonomy.

The Eastern Rosella from Tasmania was first described as *P. e. diemenensis* by AJ North in 1911.

Tasmanian Eastern Rosella
P. e. diemenensis cock

Tasmanian Eastern Rosella
P. e. diemenensis hen

European Golden-mantled
P. e. elecica
Eastern Rosella cock

European Golden-mantled Rosella—an example of selective breeding to enhance the golden yellow colouration

P. e. diemenensis

This subspecies is commonly named the Tasmanian Eastern Rosella by Australian aviculturists and is found only in Tasmania. It is reasonably common throughout the island's east. It is the largest of the Eastern Rosellas and displays larger white cheekpatches and a slightly deeper red head than the nominate subspecies. The chest and head may appear much larger than the nominate—causing the body and head to appear out of proportion.

P. e. elecica

This subspecies is commonly referred to as the Golden-mantled Rosella. Its range extends from the Hunter Valley in New South Wales, north to the Darling Downs in south-east Queensland. It overlaps with the nominate *P. e. eximius* in the Hunter Valley.

These birds have a much richer golden mantle than seen on the nominate. The mantle feathers are golden yellow with a black dot, rather than black with a green-yellow edge. The rump is blue-green and the central tail feathers vary from blue-green to dark blue. A well-marked cock will display a large red V-shaped area from the chest to the abdomen.

IN THE WILD

The range of the Eastern Rosella extends from the Mount Lofty Ranges in south-eastern South Australia to the Hunter Valley in New South Wales and west to Gilgandra and Warren in central-western New South Wales. They have been introduced to both islands of New Zealand and are reasonably common on the North Island.

Golden-mantled Rosella feeding on seed in cow manure in the wild

Their habitat includes open forest, woodlands, treed watercourses, orchards and parklands and gardens in most cities and towns throughout the range. It is not uncommon for residents on small acreages to place nesting logs to encourage them to breed. They generally prefer open plains and are rarely found in heavily timbered mountain areas where the Crimson Rosella dominates the range. Eastern Rosellas are reasonably common throughout the range and overlap with the Pale-headed Rosella *P. a. palliceps* in the north, where some hybridisation occurs.

Eastern Rosellas feed on native and introduced species of seeding grasses, blossoms, berries, nectar, insects and their larvae and the nuts of eucalypts and acacias. I have also observed these birds feeding on winter grasses, clovers and common grasses, such as couch and kikuyu, on my property during the heaviest of frosts.

Breeding generally occurs from August to February, with a variation in nesting time depending on the geographical location. Nests are located in a variety of places, including hollow tree limbs, the stumps and holes of trees, fence posts and in buildings. Up to 11 eggs may be laid, but between four and eight is more common. Incubation by the hen lasts approximately 19 days and fledging occurs approximately 35 days after hatching.

IN CAPTIVITY

Status

The Eastern Rosella is common in aviaries throughout Australia, New Zealand, Europe and the UK, being reasonably hardy and easy to keep. They are less common in the USA. Their popularity is likely to continue due to the availability of a wealth of established mutations.

The Golden-mantled subspecies is the most popular Eastern Rosella in captivity, however it is extremely hard to find in a pure form in Australian aviaries. Most specimens appear to be hybridised with the nominate *P. e. eximius*. Although I have kept many Golden-mantled Rosellas in my collection in the past, I do not have any good pure subspecies specimens as I have sold them due to space restrictions and a desire to breed 'that new mutation'—an act I now regret.

The Tasmanian Eastern Rosella subspecies is rare in captivity and likely to be extinct in its pure form in Europe.

Most European aviculturists of Eastern Rosellas prefer birds displaying a clean line across the chest to differentiate the red chest and the yellow and green abdomen. Australian aviculturists favour specimens where the red chest feathers appear down to the abdomen to form a large V-shape.

European aviculturists have established three separate colour varieties of the Eastern Rosella through selective breeding—the Green-mantled Rosella, the Yellow-mantled Rosella and the Golden-mantled Rosella—a particularly outstanding bird.

Housing

The Eastern Rosella requires an aviary measuring approximately 3–4 metres long x 1 metre wide x 2–2.4 metres high.

They should be limited to one pair per aviary as dominant birds may display aggression during the breeding season.

Breeding

The Eastern Rosella will accept various logs or nestboxes for breeding. Nestboxes constructed from 12mm plywood and measuring approximately 180mm square x 450mm high with a natural hollow spout or man-made spout—made from a similar material as the nestbox and fixed to the front—are ideal.

Eastern Rosellas will breed at 12 months of age—I have had hens that have laid eggs as early as nine months of age and cocks that have fertilised eggs at 10 months of age. However, they are generally better breeders at two years of age. These birds are prolific breeders and will double and triple brood.

Breeding generally occurs from September to January and may commence as early as July in warmer climates, such as Queensland. In my region I hang nestboxes on the first weekend of September, after which the hen will immediately start working the nest.

Up to seven eggs are laid, although I have had hens lay between four and 13 eggs. A young Cinnamon hen I had laid 13 eggs, of which 12 were fertile and 11 chicks were raised. It is not uncommon to find eight or nine eggs in the nest.

Incubation commences with the laying of the third egg and lasts between 19 and 22 days. Hens that lay large clutches, such as nine eggs, may not begin incubation until the sixth or seventh egg. Fledging usually occurs between 29 and 35 days after hatching.

Eastern Rosella chicks at 28 days of age

PRIMARY COLOUR MUTATIONS

Blue

Several blue coloured birds have been sighted in the wild. Unfortunately, none have been established in captivity.

In the mid–1990s a prominent New South Wales aviculturist obtained two 'Blue' birds and is believed to have bred several split progeny. The lack of reliable information makes it difficult to confirm if this Blue mutation has been established.

Australian Blue Eastern Rosella cock

In Europe, the Blue mutation was produced by two breeders at the same time in Germany in the early 1980s. A Mr Jentsch of Leipzig produced a Blue mutation, but it did not survive and the line was lost. Breeder Joachim Richter, of Bad Düben, also managed to produce a number of Blue birds, but these also died before reaching maturity.

In 1984 Gerhard Rübesam purchased some split birds from Joachim and produced two Blue Eastern Rosellas. Again, these birds never reached maturity. Later, Gerhard purchased all of Joachim's Blue line of rosellas and produced more Blue mutation progeny during the 1990s—all of which died. In an effort to strengthen the bloodline, the splits were outcrossed to Normal birds and finally, in 2004, a Blue cock survived and went on to reproduce.

A Blue Eastern Rosella was also bred in France in 2002, however I understand this bird never reproduced.

In 2007 I was fortunate enough to be present—along with my good friend, Bruce Brown—when a Blue Eastern Rosella cock was offered for sale and was lucky enough to be able to purchase this bird. It produced four young chicks that year, but they did not survive.

I suspect this bird to be a 'Parblue' as it has a faint tinge of red on the forehead. I will wait until an Albino has been produced before theorising further. I hope I do not have the same problems as Gerhard has had in Germany in establishing this mutation. Only time will tell.

'Parblue'

There is not a lot understood about the possible 'Parblue' mutation in the Eastern Rosella in Australia.

Several years ago I was shown a bird of partial blue colouration. It had been taken from a nest in the wild and was not a good specimen as the quality of the feathers was poor. This bird was never established and no photographic evidence was ever taken.

In the mid–1990s, Thierry Duliere of France sent me photographs of a Creamino Eastern Rosella, which were published in *A Guide to Colour Mutations and Genetics in Parrots* (2002), authored by Dr Terry Martin BVSc and published by ***ABK Publications***. However, I have no further information regarding these birds or any additional photographic evidence.

Cinnamon

This mutation is a true Cinnamon mutation and was developed in Australia by the late Alan Chalmers of Ariah Park, New South Wales, in the early 1990s. It is common in Australian aviculture. The mode of inheritance, as with all Cinnamon mutations, is sex-linked.

All the black melanin is reduced to brown and the blue is diluted to powder blue. Chicks hatch with plum-coloured eyes that darken with age and have flesh-coloured feet.

Australian Cinnamon Eastern Rosella hen

Australian Cinnamon Eastern Rosella cock

The Cinnamon, in combination with other genes, results in some interesting mutations.

I have held in my collection a bird referred to by Sindel and Gill (1999) as a 'clear-winged variant of the Cinnamon mutation'. Following this bird's first moult it emerged as a normal Cinnamon mutation.

The colours of the Cinnamon mutation across all species may fade annually, reverting to the 'normal' Cinnamon colour after the moult.

In Europe, the Cinnamon mutation was established in the Netherlands in the 1970s and appears to be the same as, or at least very similar to, the Australian Cinnamon mutation. It is common throughout Europe and the UK.

European Cinnamon Eastern Rosella cock

Dilute Series

Dilute mutations in the Eastern Rosella are a complex series of mutations. They are all recessive in their mode of inheritance and produce birds displaying normal-coloured eyes and feet. The action of the dilute gene only affects feather pigments.

Australian Dilute Eastern Rosella hen

Australian Dilute Golden-mantled Eastern Rosella cock

Dilute

The Dilute mutation has been present in Australian aviculture since the mid–1980s—originating from a wild-caught cock. Andrew Isles of Melbourne, Victoria, bred the first Dilute Eastern Rosella hen in captivity—but progress was very slow.

This mutation results in a bird displaying approximately an 80% reduction in the melanin pigment. Psittacin pigment is not affected.

The flights are grey and the shoulder-patches are sky blue—almost mauve. The tail is light green and edged in mauve. The colour of the eye and the feet do not change.

Some Dilute birds appear duller in overall colour, while others appear much brighter and have a deeper yellow colouration. This could be influenced by the base colour of the Normal bird the mutation was bred from. For example, specimens bred from the nominate subspecies will be duller in colour than those bred from the brighter Golden-mantled subspecies.

It has taken a lot of work by aviculturists to safely establish this mutation in Australian aviculture.

For many years this mutation was incorrectly referred to as 'Pastel' in Europe—'Pastel' is the name used for the non sex-linked (NSL) Partial Lutino mutation. (The mutation nomenclature system is slowly becoming more universal in all parrot species.) The Dilute ('Pastel') was the first Eastern Rosella mutation bred in Europe in the 1960s.

European Dilute Eastern Rosella

European Dilute Eastern Rosella

It is believed to have been developed by Mr Dussaud of France and continued to be developed by Dr Swanepoel of Belgium.

The European Dilute appears slightly darker than the Australian Dilute mutation and displays a melanin reduction of approximately 50%. The shoulder-patches are darker blue and the flights are darker grey than in the Australian Dilute. This 'dark' Dilute mutation could be similar to the 'Greywing' Budgerigar. Extensive breeding needs to be achieved among all Dilute mutations to determine exactly what genetic action is occurring.

Edged Dilute

This mutation is also referred to as 'Pastel' or 'Belgium Pastel' in Europe. The genetic action causes an uneven reduction of melanin and retains a greater amount of melanin than seen in the Dilute—creating an edging effect on the feathers.

The Edged Dilute mutation also occurs in the Peach-face Lovebird ('American Yellow'), the Pacific Parrotlet ('Pastel') and the Cockatiel ('Spangle Silver').

European Edged Dilute Eastern Rosella cock

European possible 'Edged Dilute' Eastern Rosella

Suffused

The Suffused Eastern Rosella is another form of Dilute. It is known by many names including 'Black-eyed Clear', 'Black-eyed Yellow', 'Dark-eyed Yellow' and 'Dark-eyed Clear'. This mutation displays a reduction in melanin by up to 90%.

This mutation was first recorded from a breeding off the coast of Wales by Peter Addison of the UK, who claims he first heard about a cock and two hens bred from two Normal birds in 1997. Peter later purchased these birds and began the long process of establishing this mutation.

The genetic action of the Suffused is similar to this mutation in the Indian Ringnecked Parrot and the Budgerigar.

European 'Black-eyed Yellow' Eastern Rosella cock

Fallow

All Fallow mutations display a red eye and flesh-coloured feet.

There have been a number of Fallow mutations kept in Australian aviaries in the past—most taken from the wild. However, none have been established in captivity. There is a cock believed to be a Fallow mutation being held in a New South Wales collection. It is hoped this mutation will be established in Australia in the future.

Sindel and Gill (1999) made reference to a Cinnamon Yellow Eastern Rosella cock, which is actually a Fallow mutation. Unfortunately, I cannot confirm if this mutation was ever established. I can find no reference to a Fallow mutation in Europe.

Australian Fallow Eastern Rosella cock

'Golden'

In this mutation the black markings on the mantle and above the shoulder-patches are replaced with a rich, golden yellow—hence the name 'Golden'. The mode of inheritance is recessive.

Juveniles display a yellow patch on the back of the head. I would suggest this is located where the green patch appears on most juvenile Eastern Rosellas. Young do not attain full colouration until two years of age.

This mutation first appeared in a clutch of Golden-mantled Rosellas in the south of France. Birds developed through the Golden-mantled Rosella form appear to be more golden in colouration. It is in the process of being developed in Europe, following extensive work by the late Dominique Lestringant of France.

It will be very interesting to observe what happens to the yellow colouration on the back when this bird is combined with other mutations such as the Melanistic and Opaline.

Left and right: European 'Golden' Eastern Rosellas

Australian Lutino Eastern Rosella hen

European Lutino Eastern Rosella

Lutino

The sex-linked Lutino Eastern Rosella is common in Australian aviculture. It results in a bird displaying an almost total reduction of the melanin pigments in the feathers, skin and eyes. Blue and black areas are changed to white and the green areas are changed to yellow. The eyes are red and the feet are flesh-coloured. There have been a number of Lutino birds recorded in captivity over the years, however none were ever established until recent times.

The first of the existing Australian Lutino birds were taken from the wild in the early 1990s from various areas—the first, typical of a Golden-mantled Rosella subspecies, was from Port Macquarie, New South Wales. The second, similar to the nominate Eastern Rosella, was from near Young, New South Wales. This bird displayed paler colouration than the bird captured at Port Macquarie. For some reason some offspring from the bird captured near Young displayed a fawn or biscuit colouration on the mantle where the black scalloping would have usually appeared in a Normal bird. They were considered by some to be 'Cinnamon Lutino' birds. However, after a number of test matings this theory was rejected and it is now considered a form of Partial Lutino.

Gerhard Rübesam reported that he acquired a Lutino Eastern Rosella hen in 1984, demonstrating that this mutation was available in Europe and bred prior to this date. The European Lutino is also a sex-linked mutation with a total reduction of melanin.

Due to fertility problems with the Australian strain, the European Lutino was established much faster than the Australian Lutino.

NSL Lutino—Recessive Lutino

Sindel and Gill (1999) reported a bird—referred to as a 'recessive Advanced Cinnamon Yellow'—originating from the wild, and was accommodated in the aviaries of Sir Edward Hallstrom before later being purchased by Ray Kerr of Wollongong, New South Wales. While a number of these non sex-linked Lutino mutations were bred it was never established.

Partial Lutino

A recessive or non sex-linked (NSL) Partial Lutino mutation appeared in aviaries in New South Wales in the mid–1990s—bred from a pair of normal-coloured wild birds. Low fertility and bad eyes made it very difficult to reproduce. However, there are a number of splits and several coloured birds presently held by breeders, which provide aviculturists with hope this mutation will be established.

This attractive mutation displays a reduction in melanin by approximately 70%. It is referred to by Sindel and Gill (1999) as 'Semi-advanced Cinnamon Yellow'.

During my research for this book, fellow breeder and close colleague Peter Rankine and I debated the possibility that the sex-linked Lutino mutation—colloquially referred to as 'biscuit-backed' Lutino—was indeed a Pallid or Lime mutation. We discussed that when combined with the blue gene, the resulting Albino mutation bird would retain traces of melanin, creating an attractive alternative to the pure white bird.

Australian sex-linked Partial Lutino Eastern Rosella

Australian Black Eastern Rosella juvenile cock

Melanistic ('Black')

This mutation is referred to as 'Black' by all aviculturists. It has a complex history within Australia. The mode of inheritance is recessive.

Most plumage is changed to black—except for the blue on the shoulder-patches and the green on the tail. The cheekpatches remain white, although many specimens display a degree of blue on, or around, the lower edge of the cheek—particularly when young.

Both the cock and hen display green and purple feathers that create a pearling effect from the chest down to the vent—more pronounced in the cock. The cock also displays more red on the chest and around the head—this can take three to four years to develop. Some hens display some red on the chest, however it is minimal compared to the cock. Interestingly, all

Australian Black Eastern Rosella hen

Australian Black Eastern Rosella cock

hens retain the red brow—perhaps there is a separate gene controlling this area.

Some of the original specimens of the Melanistic mutation displayed yellow feathers on the head around the ear coverts. Even split progeny featured some yellow on the head—much the same as the 'Yellow-headed' birds established in Australian aviculture.

Ray and Joelle Marshall developed the Melanistic mutation in New South Wales during the late 1980s. The couple purchased a coloured specimen and some juveniles from a breeder on the north coast of New South Wales and managed to produce quite a few coloured young and splits over the ensuing years.

Due to poor fertility, poor feathering and a lack of growth, this mutation was almost lost to aviculture in the mid–1990s. I believe breeders who bought this mutation from Ray and Joelle did not outcross their birds and mated birds too closely related, causing the aforementioned problems—possibly in an effort to recoup some of their financial outlay.

In the mid–1990s a young Melanistic hen was obtained by Peter Rankine and Paul Stubbington of Melbourne, Victoria. They mated her to a large wild-type cock and managed to produce one outcross split bird.

A couple of years later I purchased two Melanistic birds and several splits that had failed to produce young for a number of breeding seasons. I mated one of the Melanistic hens to a Normal Cinnamon split Opaline cock, which produced one chick—a Cinnamon Opaline split Melanistic hen. It is from these birds that most of the Melanistic Eastern Rosellas in Australia have descended.

There are a small number of Melanistic Eastern Rosellas held in collections in the UK and Europe, however their origins are unknown.

Australian Opaline Eastern Rosella cock. Note the double underwing stripe typical of Opaline mutations

Australian Opaline Eastern Rosella hen

Opaline

The Opaline mutation was first sighted by Gould in 1837 and recorded as the Fiery Parakeet *P. ignatus*. Common in aviculture, it is well-known as the 'Red' Eastern Rosella.

This stunning mutation produces a bird displaying a predominantly red body colouration with varying degrees of red in the scalloping of the mantle. In my opinion, good specimens have a pink or apricot tail. These birds also display normal-coloured eyes and the large double underwing stripe typical of most Opaline mutations. Hatchlings have white down. There is considerable variation in the colour pattern on the mantle, with some specimens displaying just a few red feathers, and others all red feathers.

The popularity of the 'Red' Eastern Rosella in Australian aviculture is due to the work of Jack Smith and his late brother Syd, both of Victoria, and Bruce Brown of New South Wales. Jack and Syd obtained their specimens in the mid–1970s in Victoria, while Bruce acquired his from the Hill End district in central New South Wales.

In Europe, the Opaline mutation was developed in Berlin in the late 1970s by an aviculturist named Spotak. It has since become well established there. In some cases I would suggest the European Opaline mutation is equal to, if not of better colour than some of the Australian Opaline examples.

European Opaline Eastern Rosella

Australian Pied Eastern Rosella cock. The pied markings indicate a possible 'Black-eyed Clear' mutation

This white-flighted Australian split Pied Eastern Rosella cock is believed to be a 'Black-eyed Clear'

Pied ('Black-eyed Clear')

The 'Black-eyed Clear' mutation is under development in Australia and is held by only a couple of aviculturists. It appears to be a recessive mutation.

The degree of pied markings may vary from a single white toenail or white feather to specimens displaying several white flights on the wings and large yellow patches on the head and abdomen. I believe these are actually visually split Pied birds—when mated together they produce a stunning bird with large areas of pied markings. The flights and the tail are snow white, the body is yellow and many have a small patch of green in the middle of the back. These birds also retain the red brow.

This mutation has all the characteristics of a 'Black-eyed Clear' as seen in other rosella species, including Yellow, Green and Crimson Rosellas. The 'Black-eyed Clear' mutation has a significant effect on the action of red psittacin pigments.

This young yellow-coloured Eastern Rosella cock of unknown classification—possibly recessive in inheritance—was not established in Australian aviculture

Australian Pied Eastern Rosella cock

European 'Dominant Edged' (left) and Australian 'Black-eyed Clear' Eastern Rosellas. Note the edged effect on the flight feathers of the European bird and the 'clear' flight feathers on the Australian bird

'Dominant Edged' ('Grey-winged and 'White-winged')

Mr Adams of Lubeek, Belgium, developed the European 'White-winged' mutation in the late 1970s. First thought to be a Dominant Pied, it currently appears to be co-dominant. The single factor specimen is referred to as 'Grey-winged' and the double factor specimen as 'White-winged' by European aviculturists. Both forms are reasonably common throughout Europe.

I have classed this mutation as 'Dominant Edged' as it does not fully classify for the Pied category. Pied genes remove all the melanin from an affected feather, whereas the dominant edged gene leaves traces of melanin in the feather—giving them an edged effect. The European birds are undoubtedly different to the Australian birds. These 'Dominant Edged' mutations display pied markings on the feet and toes—indicating that their relationship to Pied is reasonably close and suggesting a separate classification.

In Australia, a breeder in northern New South Wales is attempting to establish a mutation similar to the European 'Dominant Edged', which also appears to be a co-dominant mutation. This breeder is producing what appears to be single and

European single factor 'Dominant Edged' ('Grey-winged') Eastern Rosella

European double factor 'Dominant Edged' ('White-winged') Eastern Rosella

Examples of an Australian bred pied-type mutation similar to the European 'Dominant Edged'. This Eastern Rosella hen also appears to be a 'Yellow-headed' mutation, however she displays yellow tail feathers not seen in the 'Yellow-headed' mutation. Note the olive-green colouration on the chest and abdomen

INSET: Progeny of the hen pictured above

RIGHT: Another progeny of this Australian pied-type mutation

double factor birds. Unfortunately, the double factor birds are poor specimens and most have died shortly after fledging.

Some of these birds display an olive colour right down the front replacing the usual red, yellow and green. It is very unusual and I do not have any immediate explanations.

A Queensland breeder has also produced a possible 'Dominant Edged' in double factor (left) and single factor

In Queensland, Dave Fitch is in the process of developing another mutation that appears similar to the 'Dominant Edged'. It also appears to be co-dominant in its mode of inheritance. Dave has been working on the mutation for the past 15 years and has produced a significant number of coloured birds.

In the future it would be interesting to combine this mutation with the Australian 'Black-eyed Clear' and 'Yellow-headed' mutations to determine the presence of any genetic relationships.

'Red-fronted'

Russell Scott, of Tamworth, New South Wales, sent me a photograph of a bird he bred in 2007 displaying a full red front, much the same as seen in the Red-fronted Scarlet-chested Parrot *Neophema splendida*. This is likely to be a colour variation, which can be selectively bred to enhance the amount and extent of red colouration.

Col Gunter, also of Tamworth, has in his collection a bird with large amounts of red on the front and the mantle. He has named it 'Fiery', probably an inappropriate name considering that the original Opaline Eastern Rosella was named the Fiery Parakeet by John Gould in 1848.

Australian 'Red-fronted' Eastern Rosella

Another form of an Australian 'Red-fronted' Eastern Rosella named 'Fiery' by the breeder

'Yellow-headed'

As is the case with the 'Golden', the 'Yellow-headed' mutation does not fit into any recognised category. Only the red psittacin pigment of the head and chest is affected, which makes it difficult to classify as Pied. None of the 'Yellow-headed' Eastern Rosellas in Australia display pied markings on the feet or white on the flight or wing feathers—as are common with most Pied mutations in the rosella genus.

This interesting mutation was first established in Australia by Andy and Helen Barrow of Perth, Western Australia, in the mid–1990s.

Australian 'Yellow-headed' Eastern Rosella cock

Australian 'Yellow-headed' Eastern Rosella hen

Australian 'Yellow-headed' Eastern Rosella juvenile cock

I have been developing this mutation for a number of years. To date, fertility has been low and the mutation has been difficult to produce in any numbers. However, improvement and progress continues.

Juveniles may take at least 12 months to fully colour and they fledge with minimal red on the chest and display a yellow patch on the back of the neck—similar to the European 'Golden' mutation. Initially I considered it to be a dominant mutation expressed in single factor and double factor—and this could yet be proven correct.

However, I also consider that it may be a recessive mutation with a genetic action similar to that seen in pied-type mutations—the lightly marked birds may be visual splits. Obviously, there is still much development to be done before the genetic mode of inheritance is fully understood.

In the mid–1990s I purchased a number of Melanistic Eastern Rosellas including some splits. A couple of the split hens appeared to be the same as the 'Yellow-headed' birds. Unfortunately these two hens only managed to produce a small number of chicks before they died and, therefore, I was unable to determine the result of the genetic action.

In Europe, the 'Yellow-headed' mutation has been established for a number of years but is not common. These birds are sometimes referred to as 'Dominant Pied'.

This split Black Eastern Rosella hen appears similar to a 'Yellow-headed' bird

COMBINATIONS OF MUTATIONS

Cinnamon Series

Cinnamon 'Parblue'

This is a combination of a sex-linked and a recessive mutation.

There have been reports from Europe of a Cinnamon 'Orange' combination colour morph in the Eastern Rosella. 'Orange' is a common name European aviculturists use for the Seagreen (Parblue) mutation. It is quite attractive, however the origins are unknown.

European 'Cinnamon Seagreen' Eastern Rosella hen

Cinnamon Dilute

This is a combination of a sex-linked and a recessive mutation.

I produced the first Cinnamon Dilute specimen in Australia in 2002. Its appearance is similar to a Dilute bird, but two shades lighter overall and with plum-coloured eyes. This combination will be best realised when combined with the melanistic or the blue gene.

The Cinnamon Dilute has been popular in Europe for many years, however I suspect that it is produced in combination with the Edged Dilute ('Pastel').

At the time of publication there was no information of any Cinnamon Dilute Opaline Eastern Rosella in Australia, despite these birds having been available in Europe for many years.

Cinnamon Opaline

This is a combination of two sex-linked mutations. It was the first combination colour developed in the Eastern Rosella species in Australia. It was achieved by the late Alan Chalmers in the early 1990s.

In this combination the red body plumage colour of the Opaline is retained, black feathering is reduced to brown and the blue on the shoulder-patches and tail is also diluted. Most birds will also display the pink central tail feathers characteristic of the Opaline mutation.

This colour was first bred in Europe where it has been established for many years. Information on its background was not available, however it is possible that it originated as early as in the 1970s.

In Europe, the Cinnamon and Opaline mutations have also been combined with the 'Dominant Edged' ('White-winged') and the Dilute ('Pastel') mutations to form a quadruple combination colour—Cinnamon Dilute 'Dominant Edged' Opaline.

Cinnamon 'Dominant Edged'

This combination has been available in Europe for a number of years. The Cinnamon single factor 'Dominant Edged' specimen is referred to as Cinnamon 'Grey-winged' and the Cinnamon double factor 'Dominant Edged' specimen as Cinnamon 'White-winged'.

It is achieved by combining the sex-linked Cinnamon and the co-dominant 'Dominant Edged'.

'Yellow-headed' Cinnamon

Andy and Helen Barrow of Western Australia are understood to have produced a 'Yellow-headed' Cinnamon colour morph in the late 1990s. I cannot confirm if this combination exists in Europe.

Australian Cinnamon Dilute Eastern Rosella hen

European Cinnamon Dilute Eastern Rosella cock

Australian Cinnamon Opaline Eastern Rosella hen

European Cinnamon Opaline Eastern Rosella

European Cinnamon Dilute Opaline Eastern Rosella

European Cinnamon 'Dominant Edged' Eastern Rosella

European 'Cinnamon Dilute Dominant Edged' Opaline Eastern Rosella

Lutino Series

Lutino Blue—Albino

This mutation is a combination of a sex-linked and a recessive mutation. Typical of this combination, the Albino produces a snow-white bird with red eyes and flesh-coloured feet.

At the time of publication this colour had not been bred in Australia, however aviculturists were hopeful that this would change in the near future.

It is understood that the first European Albino was bred by Gerhard Rübesam in 2005.

European Albino Eastern Rosella hen

Lutino Parblue—Creamino

This is a combination of a recessive and a sex-linked mutation.

The action of the parblue gene retains some degree of psittacin, therefore areas of red feathers—such as on the head, chest, neck and vent—display as shades of orange or light red and cream colours.

A Creamino Eastern Rosella was bred in France in the 1990s. Little was understood about this bird and it is now believed to be extinct—I hope this is not true and that this attractive combination reappears in the future.

European Lutino Parblue Opaline Eastern Rosella

Lutino Cinnamon—'Lacewing'

This colour is a combination of two sex-linked mutations and is difficult to reproduce due to the closeness of the two genes. It is also commonly referred to as 'Lacewing' in Budgerigars.

This combination produces a bird similar in appearance to a Lutino, but with fawn markings on the mantle and the wings where black would appear on a Normal bird. The central tail feathers are a cinnamon colour.

In Australia, Greg Field of New South Wales bred the first Cinnamon Lutino in 1999.

There is little understood about the first European breeding of this colour, however they were present in aviculture in the early 1990s.

Lutino Opaline—'Rubino'

This is a combination of two sex-linked mutations and is reasonably easy to reproduce. It is without a doubt the most stunning colour of any of the rosella species.

In this attractive colour morph the body plumage is highlighted as red, the flights are white, the mantle is scalloped in yellow and red and the tail is pink.

It was first bred in Belgium in 1994 by Willy Eekeloo and in Australia by the late Alan Chalmers a couple of years later.

Australian Lutino Cinnamon Opaline Eastern Rosella

Australian Lutino Opaline Eastern Rosella

Combined with the cinnamon gene it will produce a Cinnamon Lutino Opaline. Laurie Arnold of New South Wales first bred such a bird in Australia in 2003. This bird is similar to the Lutino Opaline but displays fawn markings on the wing and the mantle.

In Europe an unknown form of dilute gene has been combined with the Lutino Opaline. The effect is very slight and probably not worth continuing.

Lutino Pied—Lutino 'Black-eyed Clear'

This colour is a combination of a sex-linked and a recessive mutation.

A Lutino 'Black-eyed Clear' Eastern Rosella—which I believe was actually a Lutino split 'Black-eyed Clear'—was bred in New South Wales in 2007.

The benefit of this mating is questionable. It may result in a clearer yellow bird—a desirable trait enhanced by some exhibition Budgerigar breeders.

The same breeder also produced a Lutino Opaline 'Black-eyed Clear'—actually a Lutino Opaline split 'Black-eyed Clear'. This mating may be worth developing, depending on the effect the 'Black-eyed Clear' gene has on the Opaline gene. The progeny could be an all yellow bird with white flights and a red patch in the middle of the back.

'Yellow-headed' Lutino

This colour is a combination of a sex-linked and a recessive mutation. There are a number of Australian breeders developing the 'Yellow-headed' Lutino and the 'Yellow-headed' Lutino Opaline combinations at present.

The 'Yellow-headed' Lutino was first developed in France in the 1990s. There is little information as to who bred it or when. It is also unknown if any 'Yellow-headed' Lutino Opaline birds have been developed in Europe—I suspect they have.

European 'Lutino Dilute Seagreen' Eastern Rosella hen

Australian Lutino Cinnamon Eastern Rosella hen

European Lutino Cinnamon Eastern Rosella

Australian Lutino Opaline Eastern Rosella cock

Australian Lutino Opaline Eastern Rosella hen

European Lutino Opaline
Eastern Rosella

European Lutino Cinnamon Opaline
Eastern Rosella

Australian Lutino Pied
Eastern Rosella

European 'Yellow-headed' Lutino
Eastern Rosella

Melanistic Series

Cinnamon Melanistic—'Cinnamon Black'

This combination colour is commonly named the 'Cinnamon Black' in Australia and was first bred by Peter Rankine and Paul Stubbington of Melbourne, Victoria, in 1997.

It was the first combination with a Melanistic Eastern Rosella anywhere in the world and created excitement among mutation breeders and genetic experts worldwide. They were excited by the degree of uncertain potential involving the combination of the melanistic with other genes in the Eastern Rosella.

When proven, the outcome was as expected. This combination reduces the usual black body colour to a cinnamon brown colour. The blue on the shoulder-patches is diluted—as is seen in the Cinnamon mutation—and birds display plum-coloured eyes and flesh-coloured feet. The hen has little or no red on the chest and head.

Visually, this colour may not appeal to everyone, however it will be appreciated in the future when it is combined with the Dilute, Pied and Blue mutations.

Dilute Melanistic—'Dilute Black'

This attractive combination mutation was first bred by Col Gunter of Tamworth, New South Wales, in 2005.

It produces a bird that retains slightly more melanin than a regular Dilute, therefore its appearance is a few shades darker.

A Dilute Black Opaline Eastern Rosella was bred by Peter Rankine and Paul Stubbington in 2008—another world first for these experienced rosella breeders.

Lutino Melanistic—'Lutino Black'

Col Gunter was the first to breed this unusual combination in 2001.

It produces a bird displaying yellow and off-white feathering over the body plumage. The mantle is slightly tinged with an olive colour.

Hens retain the red brow and some may display varying shades of red on the chest—depending on the type of 'Black' bird used for the breeding. Some 'Black' hens show no signs of red on the head and the chest—except for the brow—others will show a few scattered red feathers on the chest.

Cocks will attain the red chest—but this can take up to three or four years to fully moult in.

In 2003 Col also produced what is understood to be the first Lutino Melanistic Opaline combination ('Black Rubino') Eastern Rosella. The female progeny was particularly interesting as all hens maintained the red head, chest and abdomen colour characteristic of the Opaline mutation. Generally, they displayed yellow on the back and white on the flights.

Australian Black Opaline Eastern Rosella hen

P ODEKERKEN

Australian Black Opaline Eastern Rosella hen

Australian Lutino Black Eastern Rosella cock (left) and hen

Melanistic Opaline—'Black Opaline'

This is another Melanistic combination developed by Peter Rankine and Paul Stubbington in 2000.

This colour—my favourite to date—can produce cocks and hens with substantial colour variation. Overall body plumage colouration is black with varying degrees of red on the head, the chest and throughout the body. On the mantle there is some red scalloping and on the rump there is a variation in the degree and extent of red colouration. The tail on well-bred specimens is pink or apricot and the birds display the double underwing stripe typical of the Opaline mutation.

Also in 2000, Peter and Paul produced the first Cinnamon Melanistic Opaline combination. These birds are available in reasonable numbers in Australia. I understand this colour has also appeared in the UK and Europe—their origins are not confirmed.

In the future, the results of combining the Melanistic Opaline with the Australian Pied, and, in particular, with the Blue mutation will be most interesting. Such a bird should retain the black body colour, with the red on the head, chest, mantle, vent and central tail feathers likely to change to a white or off-white.

Australian Lutino Black Opaline Eastern Rosella juvenile

Australian Cinnamon Black Eastern Rosella cock

Australian Cinnamon Black Eastern Rosella hen

Australian Dilute Black Eastern Rosella cock

Australian Dilute Black Opaline Eastern Rosella juveniles

Australian Black Opaline Eastern Rosella hen

Australian Black Opaline Eastern Rosella juvenile cock

Australian Cinnamon Black Opaline Eastern Rosella hen

'Black Pied' Eastern Rosella

Melanistic 'Black-eyed Clear'—'Black Pied'

'Black Pied' Eastern Rosella

In 2007 a breeder in the Hunter Valley, New South Wales, produced what has been referred to as 'Black Pied' mutation. I believe this is actually a 'Black split Black-eyed Clear' and that the true Melanistic 'Black-eyed Clear' is yet to be bred. The exact outcome is questionable, however it is expected this mutation will appear similar to a regular Pied. Some differences could include darker overall body plumage colouration due to the retention of some melanin in the feathers. The green patch retained on the mantle of the pied bird may also darken to black. This combination is likely to appear more attractive in a bird displaying white on the flights than in the full 'Black-eyed Clear' bird.

Opaline Series

Blue Opaline

Gerhard Rübesam produced a Blue Opaline earlier this decade. This is the only reference I can find on this combination. In time it should prove to be a popular colour among breeders throughout Europe and Australia.

Dilute Opaline

I produced the first Dilute Opaline in Australia in 2002—a combination of a sex-linked and a recessive mutation.

One of the most attractive Eastern Rosella mutations, it displays red plumage colour on the body, head, chest and abdomen as is seen in the Opaline mutation. The scalloping on the mantle is red and the colour of the mantle, back, shoulder-patches, flights and tail is diluted.

In Europe, the Opaline has been combined with the European Dilute, the Suffused and the Edged Dilute mutations.

'Dominant Edged' Opaline ('Grey-winged' Opaline and 'White-winged' Opaline)

The 'Dominant Edged' Opaline combination was developed a number of years ago in Europe and is available in single factor and double factor forms.

In the mid–1990s the late Alan Chalmers kept an Opaline bird displaying white flights. Despite discussions with Alan before his death, he never revealed the bird's origins. This bird never reproduced and it is unknown whether it was similar to the European Dominant Edged or the Australian 'Black-eyed Clear'.

Australian Dilute Opaline Eastern Rosella cock (left) and hen

European Suffused Opaline Eastern Rosella

European 'Edged Dilute' Opaline Eastern Rosella

European 'Yellow-headed' Opaline Eastern Rosella cock

Australian 'Yellow-headed' Opaline Eastern Rosella cock

European 'Edged Dilute' double factor 'Dominant Edged' Eastern Rosella

European double factor 'Dominant Edged' Opaline ('White-winged' Opaline) Eastern Rosella

'Yellow-headed' Opaline

This interesting combination was first produced in Australia by a Queensland breeder who later sold it to breeders in New South Wales. These aviculturists are trying to combine it with Lutino to breed a 'Yellow-headed' Lutino Opaline bird.

The origins of this combination in Europe are unclear, but it has been available in France for several years.

Other Combinations of Mutations

'Edged Dilute' 'Dominant Edged' ('Pastel Grey-winged' and 'Pastel White-winged')

This European combination has been present for a number of years and can be found in both single and double factor forms.

European 'Edged Dilute' double factor 'Dominant Edged' Eastern Rosella

P ODEKERKEN

Pale-headed Rosella pair

Blue-cheeked Rosella

BLUE-CHEEKED AND PALE-HEADED ROSELLAS

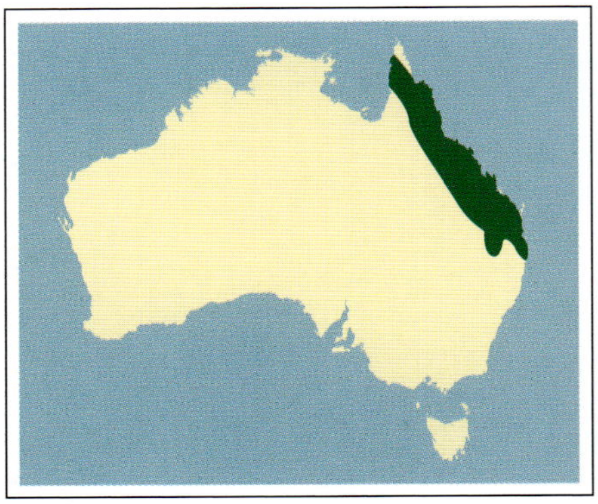

The Blue-cheeked and Pale-headed Rosellas are arguably the most complex of all rosella species. There is considerable variation in the colour and naming of the subspecies and racial variations.

As details of the wild habits, captive housing and breeding of the Blue-cheeked and Pale-headed Rosellas are similar, they are discussed below with specific details of each species following this general information.

IN THE WILD

Blue-cheeked and Pale-headed Rosellas are generally found in pairs or small family groups. Their habitat includes farmlands, savannah woodlands, treed watercourses, timbered grasslands and gardens around cities and towns. They are frequently found in sclerophyll forests and coastal heath lands.

Blue-cheeked and Pale-headed Rosellas have similar feeding habits and feed on seeding grasses, shrubs, fruit, berries, leaf buds, blossoms, nectar and insects and their larvae. They have been recorded consuming the seeds of Scotch Thistle *Onopordon acanthium* as well as Bathurst Burr *Xanthium spinosum* and Noogoora Burr *Xanthium chinense*.

Many years ago I observed and videotaped three Pale-headed Rosellas *P.a.palliceps* feeding on thistles and seeding grasses in my grandfather's vegetable garden on the Gold Coast, Queensland. These birds paid no attention to me filming and continued feeding for approximately 20 minutes before flying off.

Breeding in the wild varies due to climatic and habitat variations within the extensive range covered by these species. In the northern area of the range Blue-cheeked Rosellas breed from April to September—when the area is flush with seeding grasses following the wet season—similar to the habits of the Northern Rosella.

Nests are located in hollow limbs and branches or in holes in tree trunks—particularly eucalypts near watercourses. These birds may also nest in hollow stumps and fence posts—similar to the Eastern Rosella.

Between four and six eggs are incubated by the hen for approximately 19 days. Chicks fledge approximately 35 days after hatching.

On another occasion while purchasing birds south of Brisbane, the breeder and I were watching some young birds feeding in a paddock next to his home. He commented that they were Eastern x Pale-headed hybrids, because they had red

Blue-cheeked Rosellas in wild habitat at Watsonville, Queensland

feathers around their heads. This was incorrect, as I pointed out to him, explaining that all the young Blue-cheeks and Pale-heads that I was breeding at that time fledged with these markings and they usually moulted out during their second year.

I did have a Blue-cheeked Rosella hen that was four years of age and still carried some red feathers in her chest—but this was an exception rather than the rule.

IN CAPTIVITY

Status

The Blue-cheek Rosella is more common than the Pale-head Rosella in Australian aviculture, mainly due to the high prices the Blue-cheek Rosella commanded in the late 1990s.

There is no evidence of any pure Blue-cheeked Rosellas in Europe—there are limited numbers of intermediate birds, however, the bloodlines of these are mixed with the Pale-headed Rosella, which are kept in reasonable numbers. The Pale-headed Rosella is scarce in New Zealand and the Blue-cheeked Rosella extinct. In the USA both species appear to be almost extinct.

In Australia, a scenario common to the keeping of many native species is that the cheaper the bird, the less they are kept in captivity—many aviculturists are only prepared to keep a species they can derive an income from—a sad reality.

Housing

Blue-cheeked and Pale-headed Rosellas can be housed in a similar manner to the Eastern Rosella. They require an aviary measuring approximately 3–4 metres long x 1 metre wide x 2–2.4 metres high. As with all rosellas, house one breeding pair per aviary.

Breeding

Blue-cheeked and Pale-headed Rosellas will accept either logs or nestboxes for breeding. I have provided logs measuring 450mm long x 150mm in diameter. A hole 50mm wide was cut in the side of the log 75mm down from the top. The hens would enter the nests sideways. Nestboxes—similar to those used for Eastern Rosellas—measuring approximately 450mm long x 180mm square with a natural hollow spout or a man-made spout fixed to the front are also suitable.

Pale-headed Rosellas usually commence breeding at two years of age. However, I did have Blue-cheeks that laid and reared chicks in their first year. Generally, between four and five eggs are laid, however some aviculturists have recorded Pale-headed Rosellas laying up to eight eggs in one clutch.

Captive breeding usually occurs from July to December, particularly in the southern states of Australia. However I have kept Pale-headed and Blue-cheeked Rosellas that commenced breeding in late March and finished in December—similar to the breeding cycle of the Northern Rosella. These birds would generally lay three clutches of three and sometimes five eggs—quite extraordinary birds.

Eggs were laid at two day intervals and incubation commenced with the laying of the second or third egg and lasted approximately 19 days. After the first week or so, the cocks would enter the nest to feed the hens and just prior to fledging they would enter the nest to feed the chicks. After fledging the cocks would do most of the rearing as the hens were usually busy preparing another nest. I always removed the young at the first sign of aggression or no later than two weeks after fledging. The hens usually started laying another clutch before I could clean the nest so I just left them to it.

Fledging usually occurs approximately 33 days after hatching. Among my collection, some juveniles would at times leave earlier—at approximately 29 days, while others would wait 36 days before leaving the nest.

BLUE-CHEEKED ROSELLA
Platycercus adscitus adscitus

Other Names
Blue-cheek Rosella, Northern Pale-headed Rosella,
Amathusia Blue-cheeked Rosella, Northern Blue-cheeked Rosella
German: Blauwangensittich
Dutch: Blauwwang rosella
French: Perruche a joues-bleues or Perruche palliceps a joues-bleues

DESCRIPTION

Adult
Length: 30cm
Weight: 110 grams
Iris: Dark brown
Legs: Grey
Beak: Horn

Cock
The abdomen is blue with faint dusky edging. The chest feathers are pale lemon-yellow with dark edging—a blue tinge runs through the central area from the abdomen up to the throat. The feathers of the mantle are edged with a pale yellow-green. The blue-green back merges into a pale yellow rump. The top half of the cheekpatches are white and the bottom half are violet-blue. The central tail feathers are a dark bronze-green edged in dark blue. The outer tail feathers are dark blue. The vent is red and the shoulder-patches are violet-blue. The primaries are dark violet-blue merging to black. The scapulars are black.

© Photograph by Cyril Laubscher

Blue-cheeked Rosella cock

P ODEKERKEN

Blue-cheeked Rosella cock

Blue-cheeked Rosella hens

Hen

Similar to the cock but the chest is pale yellow and entirely separates the violet-blue cheekpatch from the lower chest and abdomen. The hen is slightly smaller than the cock and the head and mandible are slimmer.

Juvenile

Juveniles are a duller version of the adult hen, although the mantle feathers are not clearly defined. Many juveniles display some red feathers scattered throughout the head and chest.

Mature Blue-cheeked Rosella hen. Note the red flecking on the head

Subspecies and Racial Variations

The Blue-cheeked Rosella *Platycercus adscitus adscitus* was first described by John Latham as the Blue-cheeked Parrot in 1787. This specimen was collected from the east coast of Cape York Peninsula, Queensland, by Captain Cook's party. It was renamed *Psittacus adscitus* in 1790. It later became *Platycercus adscitus* but it is unclear how and why this eventuated.

John Gould described a pale yellow Blue-cheeked Rosella as the Blue-cheeked Parrot *Platycercus cyanogenys* in 1855.

The subspecies *Platycercus amathusia* was first suggested by Charles Bonaparte in 1850 and again by Gregory Mathews in 1917. It was later depicted by Joseph Forshaw as *Platycercus adscitus adscitus*.

The racial variant 'Blue-backed' Blue-cheeked Rosella cock (left) and hen

I believe this is the true Blue-cheeked Rosella and has been commonly misinterpreted by many, including myself, over the years.

The subspecies *Platycercus adscitus elseyi* is another variation and was suggested by Gregory Mathews in 1912 but not followed by others.

I believe that the subspecies *Platycercus adscitus cyanogenys,* first described by John Gould as the 'Yellow Blue-cheeked Parrot', which Sindel and Gill identified in *Australian Broad-tailed Parrots* (1999), warrants subspecies status. I believe that this subspecies is probably just one step away from the Northern Rosella in the evolutionary process.

'Blue-backed' Blue-cheeked

This variation is entirely different from all other forms of the Blue-cheeked Rosella and is the most stunning of the Pale-headed and Blue-cheeked Rosella group. The chest and abdomen is blue, almost purple, with no hint of yellow—extending up to the cheekpatches, almost to the eyes. The back and the mantle are deep blue, devoid of the pale lemon yellow displayed by *P. a. adscitus* or the rich golden yellow typical of *P. a. palliceps*. The head is pale yellow and almost white. The rump is a blue-purple. The central tail feathers are deep blue and the outer tail feathers are blue and tinted green. Specimens have been recorded in Croydon, Georgetown and Mount Garnet in Queensland.

IN THE WILD

The range of the Blue-cheeked Rosella extends from north of the Mitchell River and the Atherton Tablelands to Cape York Peninsula, Queensland. It has been recorded around Wenlock and Weipa. It overlaps with the Pale-headed Rosella at the southern end of the range.

PRIMARY COLOUR MUTATIONS

There are no known Blue-cheeked Rosella mutations in Australia. However, I did receive a poor-quality photograph of a Pied Blue-cheeked Rosella from a breeder in Europe. Unfortunately, further information was unavailable at the time of publication.

A number of juveniles I have produced in the past have displayed white toenails typical of pied-type mutations. However, I was not able to produce a Pied mutation in this species.

PALE-HEADED ROSELLA

Platycercus adscitus palliceps

Other Names

Pale-head Rosella, Mealy Rosella, Moreton Bay Rosella, Blue Rosella
German: Blasskopfsittich
Dutch: Bleekkop rosella
French: Perruche a tete-pale or Perruche palliceps

DESCRIPTION

Adult

Length: 31cm
Weight: 120 grams
Iris: Dark brown
Legs: Grey
Beak: Horn

Cock

The head is pale yellow—almost white. The abdomen and the chest are blue. The mantle is black and scalloped in rich golden yellow edging. The cheekpatches are white. The scapulars are black and the shoulder-patches are deep blue. The flights are black and edged in blue. The central tail feathers are blue and the outer tail feathers are pale blue. The rump is green-blue and the vent is red.

Pale-headed Rosella cocks

Pale-headed Rosella hen

Hen

The hen is similar to the cock, but duller overall and slightly smaller in size. The upper mandible is not as pronounced as in the cock.

Juvenile

Juveniles are similar to the adult hen but duller overall. Most display varying degrees of red feathering around the head. Juvenile cocks can be identified by a broader upper mandible.

Subspecies and Racial Variations

The Pale-headed Rosella was first described by Edward Lear as *Platycercus palliceps* in 1832.

In 1877 *Platycercus masterianus* was suggested by Ramsay for another subspecies, but this form was rejected as a hybrid.

Platycercus mackaiensis was proposed for an intermediate bird by AJ Cain in 1955, however this was not accepted.

Although there are many colour variations, there are no formally recognised racial variations of the Pale-headed Rosella.

IN THE WILD

The range of the Pale-headed Rosella is one of the largest of all rosella species. It extends north from the Clarence River in north-eastern New South Wales to the south of the Atherton Tablelands in northern Queensland. These birds can be found as far west as Wee Waa in western New South Wales and have been recorded as far west as Barcaldine and Blackall in Queensland and Bourke in New South Wales.

PRIMARY COLOUR MUTATIONS

Blue

A number of years ago, two Blue birds appeared in a nest in Australia. Paul Stubbington and Peter Rankine of Melbourne, Victoria, obtained one of these birds—a cock. Despite many attempts with different hens, so far, they have failed to produce any fertile eggs. The other bird however was fertile and did produce a number of splits. Since then, another Blue bird has been bred. With a lot of luck and a bit of hard work, this mutation may become established in Australian aviculture.

As with all Blue mutations, the mode of inheritance is recessive. All areas of yellow colour are changed to off-white. A combination with the Cinnamon mutation is under development.

Australian Blue Pale-headed Rosella cock

Lutino

Lutino Pale-headed Rosellas exist in Australia and Europe but they are in the early stages of development and little is known of their origins at this time.

As with all Lutino mutations, all melanin pigment is removed—resulting in a yellow and white bird with a red vent. The eye is red and the feet and the legs are flesh coloured. Some juveniles may display traces of red feathers around the head—generally typical of young Pale-headed Rosellas.

European (left) and Australian Lutino Pale-headed Rosella hens

European 'Edged Dilute' Pale-headed Rosella

Australian 'Dilute' Pale-headed Rosella of unknown inheritance

Dilute

Australian aviculturist, Russell Scott keeps a bird that could possibly be a form of Dilute—further information was unavailable at the time of publication.

In Europe, there is a bird referred to as a 'Pastel', that I understand was first bred by Theo Heremans in Belgium in 1996. This bird looks to be a 'Dilute' or 'Edged Dilute' mutation. The blue feathers are diluted to pale blue, the black pigment is diluted to grey and the yellow is also slightly diluted.

Cinnamon

Many years ago, the late Alan Chalmers of Ariah Park, New South Wales, bred a Cinnamon bird by hybridisation with the Cinnamon Eastern Rosella. It was impossible to differentiate the three-quarter Cinnamon birds from a pure Pale-head. I am not sure, at this stage, just what happened to these birds.

A Cinnamon mutation exists in several aviaries in New South Wales. These birds may have descended from Chalmers' original hybrids—if so, most would be more than 63/64th and as close to the pure Pale-headed Rosella as possible.

As in all Cinnamon mutations, the mode of inheritance is sex-linked. Areas of black are reduced to brown and the blue colour is diluted to pale blue. The eye is plum-coloured and darkens with age. The feet and legs are flesh-coloured.

Australian Cinnamon Pale-headed Rosella hen

European Cinnamon Pale-headed Rosellas

Australian 'Opaline' Pale-headed Rosella hen

Opaline

A number of years ago, Des Bartz of Yatala, Queensland, purchased a hen that was almost entirely red in colour apart from the head and the blue on the shoulders. It displayed the double underwing stripe typical of an Opaline mutation and white feet and toenails. According to the original breeder, this hen was bred from a Normal cock and a hen of similar colour.

The young birds she produced exhibited white feet and toenails, however they appeared very pale and diluted in overall colour. These birds are now in the care of Russell Scott of Tamworth, New South Wales and it is hoped that he will be successful in establishing this mutation in Australia.

Australian Pied Pale-headed Rosella of unknown inheritance

Pied

There appears to be two Pied mutations in the Pale-headed Rosella that have been under development in Australia for a number of years, however the exact genetic make-up is still unclear.

The first mutation displays the clear toenails and white feet markings typical of most pied birds. They can also have white feathers on the bend of the wing and pied markings on the abdomen and mantle. Most breeders assume this to be

Australian 'Recessive Pied' Pale-headed Rosella

*Australian 'Dominant Pied'
Pale-headed Rosella*

*European 'Dominant Pied'
Pale-headed Rosella—possibly
a 'Black-eyed Clear'*

a dominant mutation but I suspect that it could be another recessive 'Black-eyed Clear' mutation as seen in other rosella species. Sindel and Gill (1999) described a Pied Pale-headed Rosella in the collection of the late Colin Holt in New South Wales as a 'Dominant double factor' Pied. This was probably a recessive 'Black-eyed Clear' mutation.

The second is a recessive mutation that appears to be a Mottled. They do not have coloured feet and the young usually take 12 months to colour up. Areas of blue are changed to yellow in both mutations but of the birds that I have seen, only the dominant bird has the white flights.

Trevor Davis of Murray Bridge, South Australia has a number of pied birds in his collection. These birds may well be a combination of both mutations, as they seem to have characteristics of both. Although Trevor has been breeding these birds for many years he is still unsure of their inheritance.

There are Pied Pale-headed Rosellas present in European aviculture and they appear to be similar to the Australian 'Dominant Pied' but I cannot confirm where and when they were first bred or who established them.

'Red Suffusion'

An Australian-bred bird has been reported with unusual red colouration throughout the plumage. This could be an acquired colour change consistent with the 'Red Suffusion' seen in some other parrot species. At the time of publication this was not able to be confirmed. The three-year-old hen pictured was born with normal-coloured feathering that developed the unusual red colouration as she matured.

*Possible 'Red Suffusion'
Pale-headed Rosella hen*

Northern Rosella cock

NORTHERN ROSELLA

Platycercus venustus

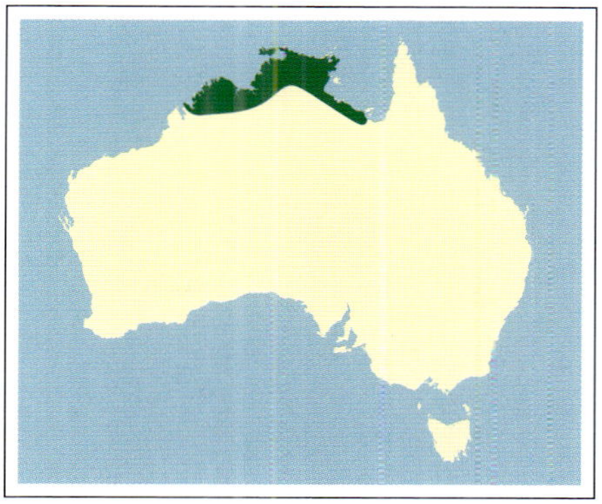

Other Names

Smutty Rosella, Brown's Rosella, Brown's Parakeet
German: Brownsittich
Dutch: Brown Rosella
French: Perruche de Brown

DESCRIPTION

Adult

Length: 28cm
Weight: 115 grams
Iris: Brown
Legs: Grey
Beak: Horn

Isolated in Australia's tropical Top End, the Northern Rosella has evolved into a particularly distinctive species. This small bird is also the least colourful of the white-cheeked rosellas and can be hard to find in the wild. Between the west and the north of the range of this species, the degree of blue and white on the cheeks may vary between individuals.

Cock

The head of the cock is black and the cheekpatches are white with a violet blue lower edge. The mantle is black and edged in yellow. The scapulars are black. The chest and the abdomen are yellow and edged in black. The shoulder-patches are violet blue, the vent is red and the rump is pale yellow with black edging. The central tail feathers are blue, washed with bronze-green and the outer tail feathers are also blue with a pale blue edging.

Northern Rosellas. Some specimens display a suffusion of red, or more commonly blue, in the chest area

Hen

Colouration is similar to the cock, although hens may have less yellow edging to the black mantle feathers. The head is also slightly smaller in size—particularly the upper mandible, which is narrower than on the cock.

Juvenile

Juveniles are a duller version of the adult. The head, neck and mantle are dull black to grey and the body plumage is dull yellow with grey edging. Some birds may display red colouration on their head and chest, but this is usually lost after 12 months of age following moulting. The underwing stripe is visible.

Northern Rosella hen

Subspecies and Racial Variations

This species was named by Robert Brown, the botanist who travelled with Mathew Flinders on his circumnavigation of Australia in 1801.

The Northern Rosella was first described as *Psittacus venustus* by Heinrich Kuhl in 1820.

This species was also once known as *Psittacus brownii* and *Platycercus browni* before the present name *Platycercus venustus* was described by Johann Wagler in 1832.

In 1910 Gregory Mathews described the subspecies *Platycercus venustus hilli* and in 1912 he described the subspecies *Platycercus venustus melvillensis* from Melville Island. These are now both classed as racial variations.

P. v. hilli

This racial variant is commonly named the Kimberley Northern or Hilli by Australian aviculturists.

It is found in the western area of northern Australia from Victoria River in the Northern Territory to the Kimberley region of Western Australia.

Kimberley Northern Rosellas are slightly smaller than the nominate and have more blue in the cheekpatches. Some birds also display some blue suffusion through the chest and the black edging is not as prevalent as in the nominate. Some specimens have a red brow.

Northern Rosellas P. v. hilli

Northern Rosella P. v. hilli hen (left) and cock

P. v. melvillensis

This racial variation inhabits Melville Island in the Northern Territory. It is smaller than the nominate and displays more black on the mantle and back.

IN THE WILD

The range of the Northern Rosella extends from the Kimberley region of Western Australia, east through the Northern Territory and into north-western Queensland. They can be found as far south as Katherine in the Northern Territory and are also present on a number of offshore islands. Cockatoo, Boongaree, Coronation, Bathurst and Melville Islands have all held small populations at times.

Their habitat includes open forests—particularly along the coastline, woodlands near watercourses and parks and gardens in Darwin. They are often found near water sources and among the eucalypts, melaleucas and acacias upon which they feed.

Northern Rosellas utilise habitat among open forest close to water sources, as seen in this photograph taken near Mataranka, Northern Territory. Note the ant beds

Northern Rosellas are sparse throughout the range, possibly due to the harsh, dry conditions at particular times of the year. They are generally observed in pairs and small groups—except during northern Australia's late dry period when they flock to drink at waterholes.

Similar to many rosellas, they feed on native and introduced seeding grasses, fruits, nectar, berries, insects and their larvae.

This species are winter breeders, therefore nesting generally occurs from June to September. Nests are located in a hollow branch or hole in a tree, often beside water and usually in a eucalypt. Between two and four eggs are incubated by the hen for approximately 19 days. Chicks fledge approximately 35 days after hatching.

Northern Rosella in the wild

Northern Rosellas will accept logs or nestboxes for breeding

Note the red feathers on the crown of these Northern Rosella chicks—this will moult out as the birds mature. This feather change is also seen in the Pale-headed and Blue-cheeked Rosella species

IN CAPTIVITY

Status

The Northern Rosella is not held in large numbers in Australian aviaries. Young do become available but are not bred in the numbers typical of Eastern, Pale-headed and Crimson Rosellas. They are rare in Europe and the USA and close to extinction in New Zealand aviculture.

Housing

The Northern Rosella requires an aviary measuring approximately 4 metres long x 1 metre wide x 2.1 metres high. All Northern Rosellas I have kept were held in aviaries 1.5 metres wide, as that was all that was available at the time.

These birds should be housed one pair per aviary. Cocks may become aggressive and it is not uncommon for them to turn on the hens and severely injure or kill them. As is recommended with all birds, it is best to house them together at a young age allowing them to mature together.

Breeding

Northern Rosellas will accept logs or nestboxes for breeding. They will breed in logs measuring 400mm with a 150mm internal diameter and hung on a slight angle. I have also had specimens breed in boxes of similar dimensions with natural spouts attached.

Northern Rosellas will usually breed at two years of age, however I have had a couple of hens lay in their first year. They are capable of double brooding—as I found when I purchased a two-year-old pair from a breeder in February 1991. By mid–April the hen had hatched four chicks and went on to produce 13 for the year, some of which were handreared and others parent-reared. The adults were prolific breeders and raised more than 40 young over the following four years.

Breeding generally occurs from March to September—although I have had hens lay in every month of the year except January. Between four and five eggs are laid and hens lay at approximately two-day intervals. Incubation commences with the laying of the second or third egg and lasts for approximately 19 days—similar to that of the Eastern Rosella. Fledging usually occurs between 30 and 35 days after hatching, or earlier during high temperatures. I usually leave the juveniles with the adults for a couple of weeks before separating them and moving them to a holding cage.

PRIMARY COLOUR MUTATIONS

Cinnamon

What appears to be a sex-linked Cinnamon mutation is under development by an aviculturist in New South Wales. All the black melanin is reduced to either fawn or brown. Typical of a Cinnamon mutation the chicks hatch with plum-coloured eyes that darken with age.

Opaline

An aviculturist in New South Wales is presently developing a bird believed to be an Opaline mutation. This mutation displays the double underwing stripe carried by most Opaline mutations and has full red frontal colouration from the head to the abdomen. It appears to be sex-linked in inheritance.

'Red-capped'

This variation was seen in specimens taken from north-western Australia—first reported by John Gould in *The Birds of Australia* (1916–17).

I refer to the 'Red-capped' as a variation as I do not believe it to be a mutation—more likely a colour variant that can be selectively bred as is practiced in the full Red-fronted Scarlet-chested Parrot *Neophema splendida*. The black feathers on the head are replaced with red.

'Red-fronted'

This variation was first identified by Gregory Mathews in the early 1900s.

A Red-fronted variation was under development by a New South Wales aviculturist for a number of years. Many Northern Rosellas display some red feathering throughout the chest area which can be enhanced by selective breeding as is practiced in the full Red-fronted Scarlet-chested Parrot. At first sight these birds appear to have been hybridised with the Eastern Rosella. However, their ancestors were legally taken from the wild population in the Northern Territory many years ago.

I can find no reference to any mutations of the Northern Rosella in Europe.

COMBINATIONS OF MUTATIONS

None known.

This pure Northern Rosella has been selectively bred to enhance the amount of intensity of red on the chest

Western Rosella cock

WESTERN ROSELLA

Platycercus icterotis

Other Names

Stanley Rosella, Yellow-cheeked Rosella, Stanley Parakeet
German: Stanleysittich
Dutch: Stanley Rosella
French: Perruche de Stanley

DESCRIPTION

Adult

Length: 26cm
Weight: 75 grams
Iris: Dark brown
Legs: Grey-brown
Beak: Grey

Distinctive colouration, marked sexual dimorphism and a quiet personality are distinguishing characteristics in this rosella from Western Australia. It is the smallest rosella and regarded by many aviculturists as the easiest to keep and breed.

Cock

The plumage on the head, chest and abdomen of the cock is red and edged in pale yellow. The cheekpatches and ear coverts are bright yellow. The mantle is black and edged in green. The shoulder-patches are blue. The flights are deep blue and edged in black. The central tail feathers are green and the outer tail feathers are green-blue diluting to pale blue with white tips. The rump is green. As some cocks age, the edges of their mantle may become red, while others may exhibit red flecking on the rump. The entire rump area may be red in some captive specimens.

Western Rosella cocks

Western Rosella hen

Hen

The Western Rosella is the only species of rosella to display true sexual dimorphism. The head of the hen is red, but unlike the cock, the chest and abdomen are flecked with green. The cheekpatches are lighter yellow, smaller and less defined than on the cock. Although the mantle is black, it may appear green with small black dots. The rump is green and the shoulder-patches are green-blue. The flights are dark blue edged in black. The central tail feathers are dark green and the outer tail feathers are blue edged in pale blue with white tips.

Juvenile

Juveniles display a green head and red frontal brow. The cheekpatches, when present, are pale yellow. The chest and abdomen are olive and flecked with orange-red. The mantle, wings, rump, tail and shoulders are dull green, as are the flights which darken to black. The underwing stripe is visible.

Red-backed Western Rosella juvenile

Subspecies and Racial Variations

The Western Rosella was first described as *Psittacus icterotis* in 1820 by Heinrich Kuhl. In 1830 it was renamed *Platycercus icterotis* by French zoologist Rene P Lesson.

The Red-backed Western Rosella was named *Platycercus icterotis xanthongenys* by Adlord T Salvadori in 1891.

In 1912 Gregory Mathews recognised another subspecies *Platycercus icterotis whitlocki* but this name was later dropped.

The Blue-backed Western Rosella was first referenced in literature by AJ North in 1912.

P. s. xanthogenys

This subspecies is commonly called the Red-backed Western by Australian aviculturists. It is not common in Australian aviculture and is believed to be extinct in Europe.

The mantle is edged in red rather than green. The rump is olive-green and may be flecked with red. The tail is blue with no hint of green and the cheekpatches are pale yellow.

Hens usually display red over a greater area of the chest and abdomen than is seen on the nominate subspecies and, unlike the cock, the mantle is grey-buff with minimal red edging to the feathers.

Juveniles closely resemble the hen but do not display as visible cheekpatches and are duller in overall colour.

This subspecies is common in drier inland areas of south-western Australia. There is much integration and subsequent colour variation in individuals where they overlap with the nominate subspecies in the wheat-belt zone of Western Australia. Here, some birds are an intergrade and may visually resemble the nominate or a variation between *P. icterotis* and *P. xanthogenys*.

Western Rosella cock, a hybrid between subspecies

Red-backed Western Rosella cock

Red-backed Western Rosella hen

Red-backed Western Rosella pair

Blue-backed Western Rosella hen (left) and cock of the Red-backed form

Blue-backed Rosella

This colour variation is referred to as the Blue-backed Western. This form is uncommon in aviculture.

Some forms of Blue-backed appear to originate from the nominate subspecies *P. i. icterotis* and others from the Red-backed form *P. i. xanthogenys*. Both sexes display varying degrees of light blue markings to the mantle feathers.

Blue-backed Western Rosella juvenile of the nominate form

IN THE WILD

The range of the Western Rosella extends from the south-western region of Western Australia, from the coastal areas and ranges of Albany north to the Moore River area.

Their habitat includes open forest, grasslands, watercourses, farmlands and occasionally, orchards. Some birds are also found in Perth suburbs.

Western Rosellas are becoming increasingly scarce throughout their range due to civilisation, land clearing and the huge numbers that have been legally trapped and exported to the eastern states of Australia over the years.

Western Rosellas feed on seeding grasses, weeds and herbaceous plants found throughout the range as well as blossoms, berries, orchard fruit, insects and their larvae.

Wild Western Rosella in a coastal area of Western Australia

Breeding generally occurs from August to December. Nests are located anywhere between 2–24 metres above the ground in hollow limbs or in the hole of a tree, usually a eucalypt. Between three and eight eggs are incubated by the hen for approximately 19 days. Chicks fledge approximately 35 days after hatching.

IN CAPTIVITY

Status

The Western Rosella is not held in large numbers in Australian aviaries, despite being the smallest and the easiest to keep in the rosella family. They are popular throughout Europe and the UK, but scarce in New Zealand.

Housing

The Western Rosella requires an aviary measuring approximately 2.5–3 metres long x 0.9 metres wide x 2.1 metres high. If longer aviaries are desired, be aware that the young can be quite flighty when leaving the nest and may become injured if allowed to generate too much speed over a distance.

Western Rosellas should be limited to one pair per aviary, as the cocks may become quite dominant during the breeding season and become aggressive towards their mates. I have observed a cock that attacked one of his daughters four days after she fledged—removing her top mandible. Remarkably she survived and went on to successfully rear young. Thankfully this behaviour is quite rare with Western Rosellas, which are generally regarded as less aggressive than other species in the genus.

Breeding

Western Rosellas will accept logs or nestboxes for breeding. Logs measuring 400mm long x 125mm in diameter with a hole cut near the top and a removable lid for inspections are ideal. Having experimented with several varying sizes, I currently use nestboxes measuring 400mm long x 125mm x 150mm square. The design includes an inspection door at the side or rear and an entrance hole measuring 60mm in diameter. The nest is fitted to the rear of the aviary in the walkway. The nest entrance is fitted with a square spout constructed of 12mm plywood that protrudes into the aviary.

Western Rosellas will breed at 12 months of age—I have had cocks fertilise eggs at just 10 months of age. It is possible for some birds to double brood but this is not common and they will rarely double brood two years in succession. Breeding usually occurs from September to December and can begin as early as late July or early August in warmer climates. Between six and eight eggs are laid. Incubation commences with the laying of the second or third egg and lasts approximately 19 days. Fledging usually occurs approximately 30 days after hatching, or earlier during periods of high temperatures.

Blue Western Rosella chicks at 16 days of age

PRIMARY COLOUR MUTATIONS

Blue

The Blue mutation was developed in Western Australia by Chris Smith in the 1990s and is well established in Australian aviculture.

As typical of all Blue mutations, it is recessive in its mode of inheritance. Plumage is white or off-white, rather than red and the cheekpatches are white, rather than yellow. Some cocks display a faint orange tinge around the forehead, which may be an indication of a Parblue mutation.

The Blue Western Rosella is quite common throughout Europe and is believed to have originated in Germany in the mid–1980s.

Blue-cheeked

Mario Carbone of Western Australia first bred this unusual mutation or colour variation from a pair of Normal birds in the mid–1990s. I refer to the Blue-cheeked as unusual because it does not comply with other standard mutations as only the cheekpatch colouration is affected.

Due to unfortunate circumstances this mutation is almost lost to aviculture as, at the time of publication, only one split hen remained.

Australian Cinnamon Western Rosella hen

Cinnamon

A suspected sex-linked Cinnamon mutation first appeared in Australia several years ago in an aviary in New South Wales. The chick hatched with plum-coloured eyes that darkened with age. The feet were flesh-coloured. Black areas were reduced to a light brown. The blue shoulder-patches were diluted to pale blue and the green areas to pale green-yellow. This bird apparently died before the mutation was established.

David Renshaw, a well-known breeder from Melbourne, Victoria, has been trying to establish a Cinnamon mutation for a number of years. Working with one Cinnamon hen—which is a very poor specimen—he has managed to produce some outcross split cocks that are of good quality and size. In the coming seasons, it is hoped that David can produce some more Cinnamon hens to successfully establish this mutation in Australian aviculture.

The first Cinnamon Western Rosella was bred in Europe in the mid–1990s but is currently uncommon there. I cannot confirm the origins of the Cinnamon Western Rosella in Europe.

European Cinnamon Western Rosella

European 'Dark Factor' and 'Mauve' Western Rosella siblings

European Dark Factor 'Olive' Western Rosella

Dark Factor

There have been conflicting reports from regions of Europe regarding the 'Dark Factor' mutation in the Western Rosella. Some breeders have informed me that it is a true Dark Factor mutation and others are of the opinion that it has been selectively bred to enhance a darker green colouration. It has been difficult to ascertain which report is correct, as I have not been able to source any quality photographs of 'Dark Green' birds to support either argument.

Some breeders do have examples of 'Dark Factor Blue' birds—discussed on page 155.

Australian wild-caught Western Rosella—possibly a form of 'Dilute'

'Dilute'

Several years ago Heiner Kastens of Germany bred a bird considered to be a recessive 'Dilute' mutation. This bird has normal-coloured eyes and diluted feather pigments. The flights are grey. Blue plumage is paler and green plumage is diluted to an almost yellow colour. Heiner has much to do to establish the correct identity and future status of this mutation.

Several years ago a bird flying with Normal Western Rosellas was legally trapped in Western Australia. This specimen displays a slight dilution of feather pigment. At the time of publication it was not clear as to what mutation this is.

Australian (left) and European 'Dilute' Western Rosellas

Recently I have received information of a possible Dilute mutation of the Western Rosella in Australia. This bird was bred from two normal looking parents and appears to be very similar to the European Dilute.

Faded ('Pastel' or 'Isabel')

First bred in Germany by a Mr Schumacher in the mid–1980s, this mutation was at first incorrectly named 'Pastel'. Mr Schumacher did not notice that the juvenile birds had red eyes that darkened during maturity. When other aviculturists started to develop the mutation they noted that the eye colour changed with age and therefore realised this was not a 'Pastel' (a name European aviculturists use for Dilute mutations). It is also incorrectly referred to as 'Isabel'. The name has since been corrected to Faded.

This is a recessive mutation and results in a small reduction in psittacin pigments.

European Faded Western Rosella

Fallow

This recessive mutation was developed in Queensland and the entire collection purchased by Col Gunter, of Tamworth, New South Wales, who is continuing to establish the mutation. At first it was incorrectly named 'Cinnamon' or 'Advanced Recessive Cinnamon', but this mutation is a Bronze Fallow.

Birds of this mutation display pale feet and red eyes which they retain as they mature. The blue, green, red and black areas are reduced in colour.

Some breeders in Europe claim that the European Fallow is lethal, while others have been successfully breeding the mutation for years. I have not been able to ascertain whether there are two different Fallow mutations in Europe or the origins of where they were first bred.

Melinda Schmitz of California, USA, bred another mutation of the Western Rosella in the mid–1990s that appeared to be similar to a Fallow. These birds were later purchased by an experienced keeper, but never established.

Lutino

The existence of a sex-linked Lutino mutation has been rumoured for years and I have only recently found proof of their survival. Hank Jonker, a well-known breeder from Western Australia, reported observing this mutation, but noted the birds died before breeding.

A couple of years ago I received reports of Lutino Western Rosellas in New South Wales. These hens were bred from split Lutino cocks and are outstanding birds. They have been paired to Blue cocks with the ultimate aim of breeding Albinos.

The sex-linked Lutino Western Rosella is reasonably common in Europe and is believed to have originated in Germany in the mid–1990s.

Lutino (Non Sex-Linked)

Sindel and Gill (1999) made reference to an 'Advanced Cinnamon Yellow' mutation that was held in a collection in South Australia that was probably a non sex-linked Lutino mutation. Unfortunately, this mutation was never established.

Opaline

In 2005 I purchased a hen that I believe was an Opaline mutation. The red plumage colour was normal and it displayed the double underwing stripe characteristic in Opaline mutations. The tail was pink and some of the mantle feathers were edged in red. Unfortunately, the bird died before breeding. At the time of publication the original pair that produced this hen had never produced another.

The Opaline mutation first appeared in Belgium or the Netherlands in early 2000. It is uncommon throughout other regions of Europe. It appears to be similar to the bird I had in my possession and is sex-linked in its mode of inheritance.

Pied

A few Pied mutations exist in Australian aviaries, however progress has been slow and this mutation is not yet established. I suspect it will prove to be a recessive 'Black-eyed Clear' as is found in other rosella species.

Split birds display breakthrough pied markings on the feet, and may also have white or yellow on the flights and patches of yellow plumage on the head, chest and abdomen.

Pied Western Rosellas have been reported in Europe since 1992 but are currently believed to be extinct. The European Pied mutation did not resemble the 'Black-eyed Clear' mutation and may have been dominant in its mode of inheritance.

Australian Blue Western Rosella cock

Australian Blue Western Rosella hens—note the lack of white cheekpatch

Australian Blue Western Rosella juvenile cock

European Blue Western Rosella

European Fallow Western Rosella

Australian Bronze Fallow Western Rosella hen

Australian Bronze Fallow Western Rosella cock

Australian Lutino Western Rosella hen

Australian Lutino Western Rosella

European Lutino Western Rosella

European Opaline Western Rosella

Australian split Pied Western Rosella cock—note the large yellow cheekpatch and yellow flecking in the head

This white-flighted Australian Pied Western Rosella mutation is possibly a recessive 'Black-eyed Clear'

A mounted European 'Pied' Western Rosella of unknown inheritance and possibly extinct

This European Western Rosella displaying pied markings is an unknown mutation

COMBINATIONS OF MUTATIONS

Blue Series

Fallow Blue

This colour was first bred by Ben Pearce in Perth, Western Australia in 2006. This combination of two recessive genes produces a light blue and grey bird with red eyes and flesh-coloured feet.

The Fallow Blue exists in Europe but it appears slightly darker than the Australian combination.

Australian Bronze Fallow Blue Western Rosella hen

Faded Blue

Previously referred to as 'Pastel' Blue, this combination of two recessive genes produces a bird slightly lighter in colour than the Blue mutation.

This colour is only found in Europe and is believed to have been first bred in Germany in the late 1990s.

Lutino Blue—Albino

Earlier this decade, Frans Nys of Belgium bred what is thought to be the first Albino Western Rosella in 2006. This combination of the sex-linked lutino and the recessive blue genes is generally one of the first combinations bred in any species featuring these two primary colours.

This all-white bird has red eyes, flesh-coloured feet and is devoid of any melanin and psittacin feather pigments.

European Albino Western Rosella

European Faded Blue Western Rosella

European Albino Western Rosella juvenile with nest siblings

European Blue Opaline Western Rosella

Blue Opaline

The Blue Opaline combination is established in some European countries, however there is little information available. It is thought to have been developed in the Netherlands in early 2000.

Cinnamon Series

Cinnamon Blue

What is believed to be the first European Cinnamon Blue colour morph was bred in the mid–1990s by Emil Antonin in Germany.

This combination of a sex-linked and a recessive gene is reasonably easy to reproduce. The blue gene removes the psittacin pigment and the cinnamon gene reduces the black melanin to a brown-fawn colour.

European Cinnamon Blue Western Rosella

Cinnamon Fallow—'Yellow'

Emil Antonin bred a bird referred to as 'Yellow' in 1999. It was almost completely yellow with the red eyes as seen in the Fallow—closely resembling a Lutino. It was reported as a combination of the sex-linked Cinnamon and the recessive Fallow mutations.

Cinnamon Opaline

The combination of the sex-linked Cinnamon and Opaline mutations was first bred either in the Netherlands or Belgium. This combination appears similar to the Cinnamon Opaline mutation in the Eastern Rosella—although it is a smaller bird.

European Cinnamon Opaline Western Rosella

European Cinnamon Opaline Western Rosella hen

Dark Factor Mutations

There is some confusion concerning the dark factor genetic action in the Western Rosella. Heiner Kastens of Germany has what he describes as 'Dark Blue' and 'Cobalt Blue' combination colours. However, I am not convinced these are the correct names for these birds. To be correct, the 'Dark Blue' is Cobalt (single Dark Factor Blue) and the 'Cobalt Blue' is Mauve (double Dark Factor Blue).

To successfully produce these combinations you would need to start with a Dark Green bird—single Dark Factor—then mate it to a Blue. The sex of either bird is irrelevant as we are dealing with recessive and dominant genes.

Once a Dark Green split to Blue bird is produced it should be mated with a Blue in the hope of breeding a 'single Dark Factor Blue'—the Cobalt. The Cobalt can be mated to another Dark Green split Blue—a percentage of the offspring would be 'Double Dark Factor Blue' or Mauve. These are magnificent birds, irrespective of correct naming.

In the mid–1990s Emil Antonin also produced what was described at the time as Cobalt and Mauve colours of the Western Rosella. I understand that these birds were selectively bred to enhance the darker colour. I cannot confirm if the birds bred by Kastens are derived from the Antonin bloodlines.

Examples of European Dark Factor Blue combinations

European Cobalt Western Rosella

© Photograph by Cyril Laubscher

Crimson Rosella cock

CRIMSON ROSELLA

Platycercus elegans

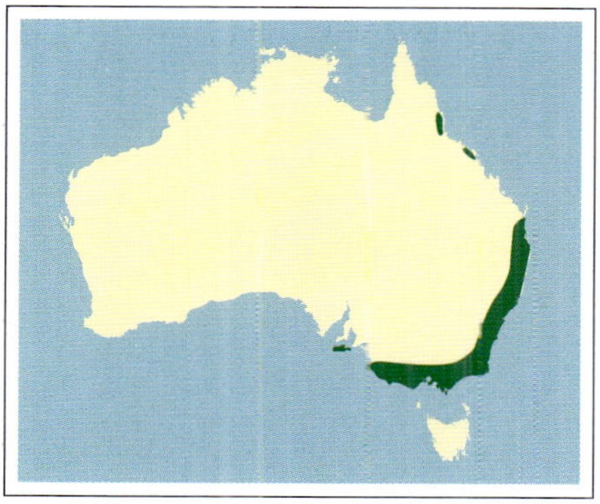

Other Names

Pennant's Rosella, Mountain Lowry, Lowry, Mountain Parrot, Red Parrot
German: Pennantsittich
Dutch: Pennant Rosella
French: Perruche de Pennant

DESCRIPTION

Adult

Length: 37cm
Weight: 160 grams
Iris: Dark brown
Legs: Grey
Beak: Horn

The Crimson Rosella is a reasonably large bird whose size increases towards the south of the range. It is a relatively uniform species displaying only slight sexual dimorphism, although juveniles display distinct variation in colouration.

Cock

The body and the head are crimson and the cheekpatches are violet-blue. The mantle and upper back are black and edged in crimson. The shoulder-patches, secondaries and underwing coverts are royal blue. The tail is royal blue with light blue edging and the underside is pale blue.

Hen

Colouration is similar to the cock, although the hen is generally duller overall. The scalloping on the mantle is darker black with crimson edging.

The hen is usually smaller in size than the cock, particularly the head and upper mandible, which are not as broad.

Crimson Rosella cock

Crimson Rosella hen

Juvenile

Juveniles all appear different—even nest mates may display a large variation in colour. Many will fledge fully or partially coloured, others will display green or olive-green colouration. The back is generally green and the front crimson, however some juveniles will display the opposite. Juveniles generally achieve full colouration at 18 months of age.

A number of years ago aviculturists incorrectly believed nominate Crimson Rosella juveniles that displayed full crimson colouration upon leaving the nest were the northern subspecies *P. e. nigrescens*.

Crimson Rosella juvenile hen

Subspecies and Racial Variations

The Crimson Rosella was first described by John Latham in 1781 as the Beautiful Lory. Then, in 1787, he described a bird he received from a Mr Pennant in New South Wales as a Pennantian Parrot, not realising that it was the 'Beautiful Lory'. Hence, the name Pennant's Rosella—the common name used throughout Europe.

In 1788, Johann Gmelin named this species *Psittacus elegans* and in 1790 Latham converted his name to latin, *Psittacus pennanti*.

It was given its current name *Platycercus elegans* in 1854 by Lichtenstein.

P. e. nigrescens

This subspecies is found in north-eastern Queensland and throughout the Atherton Tablelands between Townsville and Cooktown. It is commonly found in rainforest, particularly in elevations higher than 800 metres.

These birds are noticeably smaller than the nominate species *P. e. elegans*. Chicks in the nest are dark crimson and do not display the green plumage of the nominate. The scalloping on the mantle also varies—the feathers are much blacker with crimson edging.

Crimson Rosella
P. e. nigrescens

Sindel and Gill (1999) identified an isolated population of Crimson Rosellas around the Clark Range district west of Mackay, Queensland. Known as the 'Eungella' race, these birds were similar to *P. e. nigrescens* although slightly paler. Lendon described this population in 1973 as being indistinguishable from *P. e. nigrescens*.

This subspecies is rare in Australian aviculture and is not present in Europe.

P. e. melanoptera

This subspecies or racial variant is found only on Kangaroo Island off the South Australian coast. It is similar to *P. e. elegans* but is not as large through the chest and appears slimmer.

Aviculturist and former Kangaroo Island resident Trevor Davis believes there are three different populations of these birds on the island and that they all have their own characteristics. The eastern population is similar to the mainland *P. e. elegans*. The western population has much blacker backs than the central population.

Crimson Rosellas
P. e. melanoptera (left)
and P. e. nigrescens

In captivity this subspecies is rarer than *P. e. nigrescens* and is in danger of extinction. A concerted effort among Australian aviculturists is needed to secure their future.

Blue-fronted

Some Crimson Rosellas display a blue suffusion over the chest and abdomen—this occurs more commonly than most aviculturists realise. Blue-fronted birds do not seem to originate from any particular geographical region. I classify this as a racial variation rather than a mutation.

Crimson Rosella
P. e. melanoptera

The racial variant Blue-fronted
Crimson Rosella cock

IN THE WILD

The range of the Crimson Rosella extends from south-eastern Queensland through New South Wales, and Victoria and into south-eastern South Australia. Their range does not stretch as far as the plains west of the Great Dividing Range. They have been introduced into the wild on Norfolk Island and in New Zealand.

Their habitat includes forested areas including woodlands of sclerophyll and stringy bark and rainforest. With a general preference for coastal and mountainous areas, they are common along the east coast of Australia. They are quite common around towns and in parklands located near forests or in higher altitude regions throughout their range. They are seldom found in open country or far from timbered hills and mountains. Crimson Rosellas are frequent throughout their range.

At my property in the Hunter Valley, I have observed individuals and pairs of Crimson Rosellas flying overhead—just passing by. They are common in the mountains to the north and west of my home.

Crimson Rosella cock at a wild nest site

Crimson Rosellas feed on grasses, nectar, the seeds of grasses and trees, nuts, berries, weeds, insects and their larvae. They sometimes feed in orchards. I have also observed these birds feeding on the flowers of Scotch Thistles *Onopordum acanthium* and on seeding grasses by roadsides.

Breeding generally occurs from September to January and later in colder and higher altitudes of the range. Nests are located in hollow tree limbs and in the holes of tree trunks, usually between 2–16 metres above the ground. Between four and eight eggs are incubated by the hen for approximately 19 days. Chicks fledge approximately 35 days after hatching.

John McGrath, a well-known cockatoo breeder from Yass in the southern highlands of New South Wales, observed Crimson Rosella hens he described as half-coloured birds, breeding around his parents' home for many years. I doubt these were late colouring or young hens. This phenomena could indicate that some hens in this part of the range do not obtain adult colour. Whether this is an isolated case or not would require further investigation.

Laurie Arnold of Bathurst, New South Wales, also witnessed wild uncoloured hens breeding around his property over the years—these birds always obtained their adult plumage after the second year.

Crimson Rosellas flock to feed on seed scattered on the ground at O'Reilly's Rainforest Retreat, Queensland

IN CAPTIVITY

Status

The Crimson Rosella is common in aviaries in Australia, New Zealand and Europe. It is not common in the USA.

Housing

The Crimson Rosella requires an aviary measuring 3.5–5 metres long x 1–1.2 metres wide x 2–2.4 metres high.

This species should be limited to one pair per aviary as they are extremely aggressive.

Breeding

Compatibility is essential when selecting and establishing suitable breeding pairs. The best method for selecting pairs in most rosella species is to introduce several pairs of young, immature birds into one aviary and allow the birds to select their own mates. This method is only suitable with Normal birds, as it is impractical when selecting specific mutation pairings, as the genetics of the bird then becomes the governing factor.

A compatible pair of young Crimson Rosellas bred in Europe

When new pairs are introduced into an aviary they should be closely observed for at least a few weeks to ensure that the hen is accepted and allowed access to the feeding station. Some cocks are so domineering that they will not allow the hens near the feed station or onto a perch.

The Crimson Rosella will accept various nestboxes and logs for breeding. Hollow logs measuring approximately 750mm–1 metre long with a 200mm internal diameter and an entrance hole measuring 80mm in diameter are ideal.

Nestboxes measuring approximately 600–900mm long x 250mm square with an entrance hole measuring 75mm and a natural hollow spout or a man-made spout—made from a similar material as the nestbox—fixed to the front, are ideal. All nest facilities should include an inspection door.

Contrary to popular belief, Crimson Rosellas will breed in their first year both in the wild and in captivity. This species generally make good parents and will double brood under the right conditions.

Breeding generally occurs from September to February. Up to nine eggs are laid, but five is more common. Incubation commences with the laying of the second or third egg and lasts approximately 20 days. Fledging usually occurs approximately 35 days after hatching.

Normal and Blue Crimson Rosella chicks

PRIMARY COLOUR MUTATIONS

Lutino (Sex-linked)

The lutino gene—both the sex-linked and the non sex-linked (NSL)—removes almost all melanin from the plumage as well as the eyes and skin, but does not affect red psittacin pigments.

Juveniles display varying degrees of red and yellow colouration depending on the base colour of the bird. Some young Crimson Rosellas of the nominate *P. e. elegans* fledge completely green while others are nearly fully coloured. The lutino gene results in some young—the green birds—displaying mostly yellow colouration, and other birds displaying nearly all crimson down the chest and abdomen with red scalloping on the mantle. When fully coloured, these birds resemble large Lutino Opaline ('Rubino') Eastern Rosellas—except for the deeper crimson colouration on the body. The feet are flesh-coloured, the beak is horn-coloured and the eyes are red.

This mutation is in the early stages of development in Australian aviculture and is presently held in very low numbers by only a few aviculturists. Alan Storm of New South Wales has been developing the Lutino mutation since 1998. He has been establishing a strong and fertile strain by outcrossing the birds several times.

In Europe, the sex-linked Lutino mutation originated in Belgium and the Netherlands several years ago and closely resembles the Australian version. Some European aviculturists refer to the Lutino as 'Rubino' because it resembles the 'Rubino' Eastern Rosella in appearance. I understand this is gradually changing as when a breeding occurs from combining the lutino and opaline genes—as in the Eastern Rosella—the resulting mutation name would create confusion.

European sex-linked Lutino Crimson Rosella cock

Australian sex-linked Lutino Crimson Rosella hen

NSL Lutino—Recessive Lutino

The late Alan Chalmers kept a recessive Lutino cock that had been bred from two normal-coloured parents in the early 1990s. This mutation was stunning—at the time no-one in Australia had seen the Lutino Opaline ('Rubino') in the Eastern Rosella. This cock had poor eyesight and later died. Another coloured bird was produced which also died. I understand that a number of split and possible split birds have been paired in an effort to save this mutation from extinction in Australia—but plenty of luck will be required.

An aviculturist by the name of Mr Harms from near Münchengladbach, Germany, bred two NSL Lutino Crimson Rosellas from normal-coloured parents in 1986.

Australian Recessive Lutino Crimson Rosella cock

European Recessive Lutino Crimson Rosella

Unfortunately he died shortly after—the birds were then purchased by Günther Kosch, who established this mutation. Recessive in its mode of inheritance, this mutation has been combined with other Crimson Rosella mutations including Cinnamon, Blue, Seagreen, Dilute and Yellow.

The recessive Lutino mutation has been established longer and is more common in areas of Europe than the sex-linked Lutino mutation.

Partial Lutino ('Platinum')

This mutation is sex-linked in its mode of inheritance. The late John Leoni of southern New South Wales kept a hen in the early 1990s—described by Sindel and Gill (1999) as an 'Advanced Cinnamon'. I suggest this mutation was a Partial Lutino similar to the Platinum Red-rumped Parrot. John combined this hen with a Blue mutation before it died in bushfires several years ago. After John passed away, the remaining birds were transferred to another aviculturist who has been unable to

Australian 'Platinum' Crimson Rosella—mounted specimen

American sex-linked Parino Crimson Rosella

produce more 'Platinum' birds. However, a number of 'Platinum Blue' hens were bred from two Normal double split Blue and 'Platinum' cocks paired with unrelated Blue hens—indicating a sex-linked mutation. The resulting bird displays an approximate 75% reduction in melanin pigment. Hopefully, when this mutation is established, it will be mated to a Lutino—proving my theory correct.

It has been reported that a sex-linked Partial Lutino ('Parino') bird is under development in the USA, but little information was available at the time of publication.

Blue

The Blue mutation in the Crimson Rosella is among the most complex of all rosella mutations. It is recessive in its mode of inheritance—as are all Blue mutations.

The first Blue mutation in Australia was kept by Stan Sindel of Sydney, New South Wales. This bird was legally taken from a farm in the Tenterfield district of New South Wales in 1962.

A number of Blue birds have bred in the wild and some were legally imported into Australia in the early 1990s. Although they are being bred in reasonable numbers in captivity, they are not classified as common.

True Blue mutations are devoid of all red and yellow psittacin pigments. Therefore, the black and blue areas remain the same colour and the crimson areas are changed to light grey or off-white.

In Europe, the Blue Crimson Rosella is reported to have originated in Germany in the early 1970s and were quickly bought by aviculturists in Belgium and the Netherlands.

Australian Blue Crimson Rosella hen

Australian Blue Crimson Rosella cock

European Blue Crimson Rosella

Parblue Series

The parblue gene is part of the blue gene family. However, while the blue gene removes all red and yellow pigments, the parblue gene removes only part of the red and yellow pigments.

The parblue gene has incorrectly been referred to as dominant in the past. It is recessive in its mode of inheritance in Normal or wild-type birds, and dominant when mated to the Blue mutation—producing Parblue birds.

There are three distinct Parblue mutations in Australia.

Seagreen

This mutation produces a bird with approximately 20% reduction in psittacin pigment, diluted evenly throughout the body. The action of the gene retains the blue and black colouration, producing a striking bird—particularly when still displaying juvenile plumage. The head and chest are bright orange and the abdomen and the mantle display patches of blue colour. Mature birds appear similar to orange Adelaide Rosellas.

In Australia, the first Seagreen' mutation was bred by Laurie Arnold of New South Wales in 2004. This bird was bred from a Blue cock and a normal-coloured hen—possibly split for Blue. Some aviculturists have named the young produced as 'ParblueBlue'.

Although it appears identical, this mutation may have been bred differently than the Seagreen in Europe. I have received conflicting reports as to who was the first to breed the 'Orange' mutation in Europe in the early 1990s. These 'Orange' birds are increasingly being referred to as Seagreen in Europe.

This mutation has been combined with most of the Crimson Rosella mutations including Lutino, Dilute, Cinnamon, Yellow and Pied. The establishment of the Seagreen will be important to Australian aviculturists as it will form the basis for many new combination colours.

Aqua

This mutation produces a bird with approximately 50% reduction in psittacin pigment.

It originated in southern Queensland in the mid–1990s and is currently being developed in New South Wales. It is a striking mutation that produces a bird with salmon colouring on the front and royal blue on the back.

After several years of outcrossing to Normal birds to establish a good strain of split birds, the original Aqua cock was paired to a split Turquoise hen and a single chick was raised. This chick was a Parblue—confirming at least two of the parblue genes are multiple alleles on the same locus in the Australia breeding.

Turquoise

This mutation produces a bird similar to the Blue mutation and with approximately 80% reduction in psittacin pigment. Specimens display a slight orange tinge to the head and down the chest and abdomen.

The Turquoise Crimson Rosella originated from a collection in the southern highlands of New South Wales in the mid–1990s. Although numbers are sufficient to class it as secure, this mutation is far from common. It will be particularly useful when combined with Lutino to produce Creamino and also when combined with Cinnamon and 'Platinum'.

In Europe there appears to be a Parblue mutation similar to Australia's Turquoise—known as 'Pastelblue'. However, in accordance with the recommended international naming system, this name should be discontinued. Unfortunately, little is understood about this European bird—it appears to be rare.

Australian 'Seagreen'
Crimson Rosella juvenile

European Seagreen Crimson Rosella

Australian 'Seagreen' (left) and
Turquoise Crimson Rosella juveniles

European Seagreen Crimson
Rosella juvenile

Australian Aqua Crimson Rosella juvenile

Australian Turquoise Crimson Rosella hen (left) and cock

The European 'Pastelblue'—a Parblue mutation—is similar to the Australian Turquoise Crimson Rosella. The name Pastelblue should be discouraged whenever possible

Australian Aqua Crimson Rosella cock

Australian AquaTurquoise Crimson Rosella cock

Cinnamon

This mutation is a typical sex-linked Cinnamon mutation. The chicks display plum-coloured eyes that darken with age. The black pigments are reduced to brown and the blue are diluted to light blue. The feet are flesh-coloured.

Although quite a number of Cinnamon Crimson Rosellas have been held in captivity in Australia in the past, none have been established in large numbers. Most of these birds have been taken from the wild and some possibly crossed with the Cinnamon Adelaide Rosella.

Dedicated rosella aviculturists presently hold a small number of pure Cinnamon Crimson Rosellas. Hopefully, over the next few years these birds will become more available and add another dimension to mutation breeding possibilities.

Peter Rankine and Paul Stubbington of Melbourne, Victoria, are in the process of establishing a Cinnamon mutation.

Australian Cinnamon Crimson Rosella juvenile hen

European Cinnamon Crimson Rosella

Australian Cinnamon Crimson Rosella hen

The Cinnamon mutation is understood to have appeared shortly after the Blue mutation in Europe many years ago. It is common throughout Europe and closely resembles the Australian version.

Yellow

This mutation is recessive in its mode of inheritance and produces a bird displaying normal-coloured eyes and flesh-coloured feet. The cheekpatches are white and washed with pale blue.

This is not an easy mutation to classify correctly as it does not easily fit into a recognised category such as 'Suffused' or 'Black-eyed Clear'. It is possibly a 'Suffused' mutation—a form of Dilute. The gene action reduces a large amount of melanin pigment, however there appears to be great variation in the amount of red psittacin loss which is common with Black-eyed Clear mutations.

Some specimens display traces of red colouration around the head and the vent, while others display almost completely red fronts. The blue colour is diluted and the flights and tail are reduced to grey. Most birds are selectively bred to reduce the amount of red psittacin.

This mutation has been established in Europe for many years. It is reported as being first bred by Mr Verheijen in the south of the Netherlands in the early 1970s. The first few birds did not survive. Later, Mr Ververgaert and Mr van Deyck purchased some specimens and Mr van Deyck went on to successfully fledge the first Yellow Crimson Rosella. Günther Kosch of Radicke bred the first Yellow Crimson Rosellas in Germany in 1979.

In Europe, the Yellow mutation has been combined with most other mutations in the Crimson Rosella.

European Yellow Crimson Rosella

Sindel and Gill (1999) have described a bird similar to the European Yellow as a 'Dilute Cinnamon Yellow'. However, I can find no further information on this bird. They also described another bird as an 'Advanced Dilute Yellow', which also appeared to closely resemble the European Yellow. Again, I was unable to find further information prior to publication.

In late 2007 I received a photograph of a 'Yellow' bird from a breeder in New South Wales—similar to the European Yellow. It was a mature cock displaying black eyes and normal-coloured feet. The majority of the mantle and back was devoid of any red pigment. The bird did not appear to be in good condition and much work was needed to ensure its survival.

Australian 'Yellow' Crimson Rosella—possibly a 'Suffused' mutation

European Yellow Crimson Rosella

European Yellow Crimson Rosella cock

Fallow

This mutation is recessive in its mode of inheritance. The eye colour is red in the adult bird.

The Fallow family of mutations are generally divided into four different groups according to changes to the melanin in a bird. These groups are: Ashen Fallow for reduction to 'grey', Dun Fallow for reduction to 'grey-brown', Bronze Fallow for reduction to 'brown' and Pale Fallow for reduction to 'pale brown'.

A Fallow Crimson Rosella cock was reared from two normal-coloured parents in the New England area of New South Wales several years ago. Sindel and Gill (1999) listed it as a 'Recessive Cinnamon'. This bird appeared to be a typical Fallow displaying a pale-coloured beak and feet. The black colour is reduced to brown or fawn and the blue colour is diluted. The correct classification of this Fallow needs further investigation. However, there is little understood about it and I cannot confirm if it was ever established.

Australian Fallow Crimson Rosella hen

European Fallow Crimson Rosella cock (above) and hen (below)

An aviculturist in New South Wales held a bird I initially identified as a Partial Lutino mutation after viewing photographs of the specimen. However, upon viewing and photographing the bird myself, I now believe it is a Fallow mutation—possibly a Bronze Fallow. This bird displays flesh-coloured feet and bright red eyes. It has bred a number of split progeny, however no other coloured birds had been produced at the time of publication. It is likely to be recessive in its mode of inheritance.

In Europe there are two Fallow mutations—referred to as 'Bronze' Fallow and 'Clear' Fallow by European aviculturists. According to aviculturists in Belgium, these two Fallow mutations are almost identical—the eye colour of the 'Clear' Fallow is a brighter red than the 'Bronze' Fallow, resembling that of the eye colour of a Lutino bird. However, on both birds the black melanin is reduced to brown and the blue diluted to pale blue. Adult specimens retain the same eye colour they have at hatching. More investigation is required into these two mutations to determine their correct classification.

When two different Fallow mutations occur, their existence can be confirmed by mating them together—the progeny being all normal-coloured young split for both Fallow types. Some aviculturists and researchers believe at least one of the fallow genes is actually an allele of the NSL Lutino. Test mating in Cockatiels between the Bronze Fallow and the NSL Lutino have proven this theory correct. It would be interesting to test mate these two Fallows to the NSL Lutino to see the results. This may already have been done, but I was unaware of the fact at the time of publication.

Australian Dilute Crimson Rosella cock

European Dilute (European 'Pastel') Crimson Rosella

Dilute

This mutation is recessive in its mode of inheritance. A Dilute Crimson Rosella developed in the late 1990s is held in a New South Wales collection. This bird displays normal-coloured eyes and feet. The mantle, flights and tail are diluted from black to grey. The cheekpatches, shoulder-patches and tail are diluted from blue to mauve.

Sindel and Gill (1999) published a photograph of a Dilute Crimson Rosella hen displaying slightly diluted feathers. The eyes and the feet are normal-coloured. I doubt it is a Dilute as the black areas are diluted to brown, rather than grey. It is understood this bird never reproduced.

In Europe, the 'Pastel' mutation is actually another form of Dilute. It is believed to have been developed in Belgium in the mid–1980s. This bird displays normal-coloured eyes and feet. There appears to be a small degree of difference in the amount of dilution in some of the birds. The black colour on the mantle, flights and tail are diluted to grey and the blue is also diluted. It appears to be a typical Dilute mutation, although slightly darker than the Australian Dilute mutation.

Pied

Although Pied Crimson Rosellas have been present in Australian aviculture for many years, they have not been established in large numbers.

These birds generally display pied markings on the feet and white flights. Crimson feathering is replaced with patches of yellow colour, which varies from a few yellow feathers to large sections of bright, creamy yellow areas around the head and abdomen. They can also display white feathers on the bend of the wing and the cheekpatches are completely or partially white in some specimens.

Australian split Pied Crimson Rosella cock (above) and juvenile cock (right)—possibly a recessive Black-eyed Clear mutation

European Pied Crimson Rosella of unknown classification

European 'Dominant Pied' Crimson Rosella

European 'Dominant Pied' Crimson Rosella juveniles

I believe this mutation is a recessive 'Black-eyed Clear'. Many aviculturists believe it is a dominant mutation—as when a Pied is mated to a Normal bird, some offspring can display pied markings. However, I believe these birds are, in fact, 'visual split' Pieds.

When two recessive split Pieds are mated, the outcome is a 'Clear' Pied—unlike most dominant Pied matings where there is only a slight colour difference between single factor and double factor birds. In the past this mutation was sometimes referred to as a 'Reverse Pied'.

In 2003 I bred a chick from two birds displaying patches of yellow colour and white flights. It displayed snow-white down and clear feet—as seen in a Lutino. Unfortunately the chick did not survive beyond 17 days—however I believe it could have been a 'Clear' Pied as it was completely different in appearance to any chicks that I have ever bred from this mating. Both parents of this bird have since died, but I do possess other siblings that display similar markings. There are presently sufficient numbers of these 'split Pied' birds to be secure. Hopefully it will only be a matter of time before a full Pied specimen is developed.

European Pied—a possible 'Black-eyed Clear' Crimson Rosella

In Europe there is a mutation named 'Dominant Pied' or 'Yellow-headed Pied' that appears identical to the Australian Pied. I suspect it is a recessive mutation and that the split birds will display the breakthrough pied markings typical of the Australian birds. Günter Ballon of Germany is reported to have bred a completely 'Clear' Pied bird from these 'Dominant Pieds'—indicating the mode of inheritance is recessive or at least that there are some hidden recessive genes involved.

In Europe, there is another recessive Pied mutation that displays more pied areas than the 'Dominant Pied'. From information supplied to me by European aviculturists this mutation is possibly a 'progressive pied'—it develops increased pied markings after each annual moult—similar to the Pied Pale-headed Rosella. However, this 'progressive' trait may be simply due to the change in plumage colour from green to red as a Crimson Rosella matures. It is a stunning mutation—particularly when combined with the Blue mutation.

'Dominant Edged'

In Europe, there are one or two mutations referred to as 'Recessive Pied' and/or 'White-winged' that may be 'Dominant Edged' mutations. They display similar edging to the wings and tail as is seen in the Dominant Edged Eastern Rosella. More investigation is required to correctly identify this mutation.

'Dark Factor'

The mode of inheritance of dark factor genes is co-dominant—the single factor producing the Dark Green and the double factor producing the Olive.

German aviculturists believe they have a dark gene that produces single and double factor birds—referred to as 'Olive'. I could only find reference to this mutation in Germany and Austria. It appears that this 'Dark Factor' is only evident in young birds

Examples of possible 'Dominant Edged' mutations in the Crimson Rosella bred in Europe

or when combined with mutations such as Cinnamon, Yellow, Dilute ('Pastel') and Seagreen ('Orange').

Young 'Dark Factor' Crimson Rosellas would display a darker green colouration and, as this colour is replaced with crimson as the bird matures, it would disappear—except for the blue areas, which would darken slightly.

In 2006, I bred a Crimson Rosella cock unlike any Crimson Rosella I have ever observed. The mantle is dark green and the cheekpatches and shoulder-patches are a darker blue than that of its nest mates. Prior to publication I could not confirm if this bird was similar to the European mutation.

Australian Crimson Rosella juvenile cock—a possible 'Dark Factor' mutation

Opaline

All Opaline mutations have proven to be sex-linked in their mode of inheritance.

Several years ago I viewed a deceased bird, which appeared to be an Opaline mutation. This bird of normal colouration displayed a pink tail and a double underwing stripe typical of an Opaline. I believe the aviculturist responsible has since been unable to reproduce this mutation.

An experienced New South Wales aviculturist possesses a bird I thought was an Opaline, but it does not display the typical double underwing stripe. At the time of publication I was unsure what type of bird this is, or if it is a mutation at all.

Roy Nichols of New Zealand reported a bird held by a colleague that appears similar to the Australian mutation—except it displays the typical underwing stripe.

An Opaline bird has been reported in Belgium, however the only information is a reference made by Herman Zomer (2006) to an 'Opaline Blue'. This is quite an attractive mutation.

A possible 'Opaline' Crimson Rosella bred in Australia

A possible 'Opaline' Crimson Rosella bred in New Zealand

COMBINATIONS OF MUTATIONS

Due to the number of primary mutations in the Crimson Rosella, the number of possible secondary and tertiary combinations exceeds 300—far too many to list in detail. Following is a summarised description of the main established combination colours and details of further combination possibilities. To avoid confusion, genetic names are used for the combination colours—with the exception of a couple that are well recognised throughout the world—such as Albino (Lutino Blue) and Creamino (Lutino Parblue).

Lutino Series

There are two Lutino mutations in the Crimson Rosella—a sex-linked and a recessive or non sex-linked (NSL). Both mutations are of similar appearance, however the mode of inheritance and breeding outcomes are different.

Lutino Blue—Albino

This combination produces a white, or nearly all white, bird. Remember that the lutino gene cannot completely remove all traces of melanin from a bird—otherwise it would not survive. This explains why faint tinges of blue or green colouration are seen when Lutino or Albino birds are viewed in a particular light.

The lutino gene action removes grey, black and brown colours from the bird while the blue gene removes red and yellow colours—producing an Albino. These birds have red eyes and flesh-coloured feet.

In Europe, the Albino exists in sex-linked and NSL matings. This mutation has not been bred in Australian aviculture.

To produce tertiary colours, the Albino and the Cinnamon mutations can be combined to produce an Albino Lacewing. This bird is basically all white with traces of brown on the shoulder-patches and on the mantle where the black melanin would normally appear.

Lutino Parblue—Creamino

All the Parblue combination mutations ie Turquoise, Aqua and Seagreen have been included in this section.

The blue gene removes all red and yellow pigments but the parblue gene only removes a portion of these pigments from the plumage. This is why birds display only a slight reduction in the red pigment as is seen in the Seagreen mutation, and other birds display only a faint tint of red or orange as seen in the Turquoise mutation.

The combination of a parblue and a lutino gene produces a bird devoid of grey, black or brown colour, but which still displays traces of red pigments. The colour of this combination can vary, depending on the aviculturist's preference as to which Parblue mutation is used in the mating.

In Europe, the Lutino Seagreen mutation is well established. It does not exist in Australian aviculture.

The cinnamon gene can be combined to produce a Cinnamon Creamino in various shades. The European Yellow mutation can also be combined to slightly alter the amount of red or orange plumage colour on the body.

Lutino Cinnamon—'Lacewing'

Strangely, when the sex-linked lutino and cinnamon genes are combined, the lutino gene fails to remove all traces of melanin, resulting in a generally white bird displaying traces of brown on the shoulder-patches and the mantle where the black colour would normally appear. This combination is present in the Eastern Rosella in Australia.

In the future it will be possible to breed this colour in Crimson Rosellas in Australia.

This combination is believed to have only been bred in Europe using the NSL Lutino.

European NSL
Lutino Cinnamon
Crimson Rosella cock

Lutino Pied

This may not be a typical combination to pursue, however I believe that it may be worth trying as it is likely to produce very interesting results—due to the amount of red pigmentation present in the Crimson Rosella and the effect of the pied gene on this species. Either of the lutino genes—sex-linked or recessive—and the pied genes—recessive or dominant—could be used.

Various tertiary colours may be achieved by combining Cinnamon to produce Pied 'Lacewing', with any parblue gene to produce Pied Creamino and with the dark factor gene.

European NSL Lutino Cinnamon Blue
Crimson Rosella cock

Partial Lutino (Sex-linked)

Platinum Blue

In 2005, an aviculturist on the south coast of New South Wales produced what could be the first 'Platinum Blue' Crimson Rosella. This is a combination of the recessive Blue and the sex-linked 'Platinum' mutations. It produces a bird that displays light shades of blue, green and silver colour throughout the body plumage.

In 2006, another aviculturist produced more of these birds. This colour is likely to be a key combination for Australian aviculturists over the next 10 years.

More diverse colours can also be achieved with this combination through the addition of any parblue gene to produce Platinum Turquoise, Platinum Aqua and Platinum Seagreen. It may also be combined with Cinnamon to produce Cinnamon Platinum, with Dilute to produce Dilute Platinum, with Fallow to produce Fallow Platinum and with Yellow to produce Yellow Platinum.

Australian Platinum Blue
Crimson Rosella hen

European Albino Crimson Rosella

European Albino Crimson Rosella hen

European Blue Opaline Crimson Rosella

European Lutino Turquoise Crimson Rosella—known as Lutino 'Pastelblue' by European aviculturists

European Lutino Seagreen Crimson Rosella

European Lutino Seagreen Crimson Rosella

European Lutino Seagreen Crimson Rosella

European Lutino Yellow Seagreen Crimson Rosella

'Yellow' Series

In Europe, this recessive mutation acts as the base for combining many other Crimson Rosella mutations. It has not been confirmed in Australia, therefore the following combinations are limited to Europe.

Yellow Blue—White

This colour is a combination of two recessive genes. It is quite popular in Europe and is referred to as 'Silver' or 'White'. Using the international naming system, the correct term for this combination is White. 'Silver' is reserved for the Dilute Blue combination.

Yellow Parblue

Any parblue gene such as Turquoise, Aqua or Seagreen may be combined with the Yellow mutation. The yellow will remain unchanged, however the red pigments will vary depending on which parblue gene is used. It has been combined with Fallow to produce Fallow Yellow Seagreen.

Cinnamon Series

The cinnamon gene is useful in any species. It can be used in combination with all other primary mutations.

Cinnamon Blue

This colour is a combination of recessive and sex-linked genes and is commonly named 'Ivory'.

The blue gene removes all psittacin pigment while the cinnamon gene reduces the black melanin to brown.

The first Cinnamon Blue Crimson Rosella in Australia is believed to have been bred by Gerry Rutte in 2006. Peter Rankine and Paul Stubbington produced another Cinnamon Blue in 2008. This combination has been available in Europe for a number of years.

It can be combined with Pied to produce Cinnamon Blue Pied, with Fallow to produce Cinnamon Fallow Blue and with Dilute to produce Cinnamon Dilute Blue.

Cinnamon Parblue

This colour is a combination of sex-linked and recessive genes. A relatively easy combination to develop, I believe it will be one of the next colours to be produced in Australia in the future. Any parblue gene can be used—the Seagreen, Aqua or Turquoise.

The cinnamon gene reduces the black areas to brown and the parblue gene dilutes the red areas to orange or light red—depending on which parblue gene is used.

The dilute gene can be combined to produce Cinnamon Dilute Seagreen and Cinnamon Dilute Turquoise.

Combined with the dominant or recessive pied gene it will produce Cinnamon Seagreen Pied and Cinnamon Turquoise Pied.

Cinnamon Dilute

This colour is a combination of recessive and sex-linked genes.

Similar to the action seen in the Cinnamon Yellow combination, the cinnamon gene reduces any traces of melanin from the plumage—making the Dilute mutation appear cleaner in colour.

This combination is more commonly combined with other primary mutations such as Blue to produce Cream and with the Parblue mutations.

Cinnamon Yellow

This combination has been present in Europe for a number of years and involves the combination of sex-linked and recessive genes. The action of the cinnamon gene reduces any melanin left in the feathers—producing a bird displaying more yellow overall.

Combination with Fallow will produce Cinnamon Fallow Yellow, with Blue will produce

Cinnamon Yellow Blue, and with a parblue gene will produce Cinnamon Yellow Seagreen or Cinnamon Yellow Turquoise—depending on the parblue gene combined.

Cinnamon Fallow

This attractive colour is a combination of recessive and sex-linked genes.

The blue plumage is lightened to a pale blue colour. The black areas on the wings, mantle and tail are reduced to a red-brown colour.

It may be combined with the yellow and blue genes to produce Cinnamon Fallow Yellow Blue.

Dilute Series

Dilute Blue—'Silver'

This is a combination of two recessive genes. It is commonly named 'Silver'. The blue gene removes red pigments resulting in a bird displaying off-white or light grey in these areas. The dilute gene dilutes this colour further to a silver colour.

Combined with Cinnamon it will produce the cream coloured Cinnamon Dilute Blue and with Fallow it will produce Fallow Dilute Blue.

Dilute Parblue

As mentioned above the blue gene removes the red pigments and the parblue gene only removes part of the red pigments depending on which parblue gene is combined.

The dilute gene dilutes all the black, brown and grey pigments from the feather. This produces a bird that displays varying degrees of red and orange colour. The flights are diluted to grey and the blue areas on the shoulder-patches, cheekpatches and tail are diluted to pale blue.

It can be combined with the Cinnamon, Fallow and Yellow mutations.

Dilute Yellow

This colour is the combination of two recessive mutations and although it is difficult to justify, benefits are realised when they are used in conjunction with a third mutation—such as Blue to produce Dilute Yellow Blue or Fallow to produce Dilute Fallow Yellow.

This colour may be combined further with the Dark Factor and the Seagreen to produce subtle changes.

Fallow Series

In all Fallow mutations the bird retains red eyes and flesh-coloured feet.

Fallow Blue

This colour is a combination of two recessive genes. The action of the blue gene removes the red pigments and the action of the fallow gene reduces the black colour to brown. The blue areas are also lightened to pale blue.

Dilute may be combined to produce an attractive tertiary colour.

Fallow Seagreen

This colour is a combination of two recessive genes. It produces a bird displaying orange body plumage, with the black colour reduced to brown and the blue areas diluted to pale blue.

Fallow Yellow

This colour is the combination of two recessive mutations—of minor benefit on its own but most effective when combined with Blue to produce Fallow Yellow Blue, with Cinnamon to produce Cinnamon Fallow Yellow and with Seagreen to produce Fallow Yellow Seagreen. This colour may also lead to some interesting tertiary and quad combinations such as Cinnamon Fallow Yellow Blue.

European Cinnamon Yellow Seagreen Crimson Rosella hen

European Yellow Seagreen Crimson Rosella

European Fallow Yellow Seagreen Crimson Rosella

European Dilute Yellow Seagreen Crimson Rosella juvenile

European Dilute Yellow Seagreen Crimson Rosella

European Cinnamon Yellow Seagreen Crimson Rosella hen

European Cinnamon Yellow Blue
Crimson Rosella

European Cinnamon Yellow Turquoise
Crimson Rosella

European Yellow Blue
Crimson Rosella

European Dilute Yellow Blue
Crimson Rosella

European Cinnamon Blue Crimson Rosella

European Cinnamon Blue Crimson Rosella

Australian Cinnamon Parblue Crimson Rosella juvenile

Australian Cinnamon Parblue Crimson Rosella

Australian Cinnamon Blue Crimson Rosella juvenile hen

European Cinnamon Fallow Crimson Rosella

European Cinnamon Fallow Blue Crimson Rosella cock

European Cinnamon Seagreen Crimson Rosella

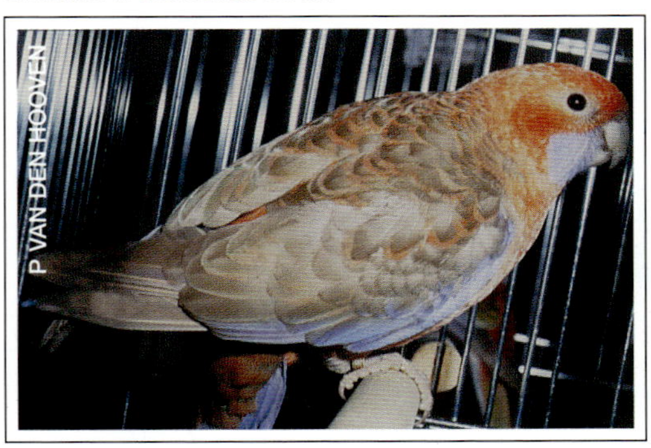

European Cinnamon Seagreen Crimson Rosella

European Cinnamon Seagreen Crimson Rosella

European Cinnamon Yellow Crimson Rosella

European Cinnamon Dilute Blue Crimson Rosella

European Cinnamon Fallow Yellow Crimson Rosella

European Cinnamon Fallow Yellow Blue Crimson Rosella

European Dilute Seagreen
Crimson Rosella

European Dilute Blue
Crimson Rosella

European Dilute Yellow
Crimson Rosella

European Fallow Blue Crimson Rosella

European Fallow Seagreen Crimson Rosella

European Fallow Blue Crimson Rosella cock

European Dilute Fallow Blue Crimson Rosella

Pied Series

As there are two modes of inheritance for the Pied mutation—dominant and recessive—aviculturists must be aware of the relevant genetic action when combining the pied gene with other mutations.

Blue Pied

Australian aviculturists are working on developing the combination of blue and pied genes to establish a 'Blue Pied' colour morph—a stunning result. It is far easier to produce this combination using a dominant pied rather than a recessive pied gene.

The blue gene removes all red pigmentation and the pied gene removes areas of blue leaving them white intermittently.

Blue Pied can be combined with Cinnamon to produce Cinnamon Blue Pied and with Fallow to produce Fallow Blue Pied and possibly Cinnamon Fallow Blue Pied. The latter would be an extremely difficult bird to produce with a recessive Pied gene as it would require the combination of three recessive genes and one sex-linked gene. Combining the dominant pied gene, making the combination of two recessive, a dominant and a sex-linked gene, would make this combination slightly easier to develop.

Parblue Pied

This combination is produced using a similar approach as with the Blue Pied. The amount of red and orange pigmentation retained in the bird depends on which parblue gene is combined.

The Parblue Pied is an attractive combination colour and can be combined with Cinnamon to produce Cinnamon Parblue Pied or with Fallow to produce Fallow Parblue Pied.

Cinnamon Pied

This colour is the combination of a sex-linked and a recessive or dominant gene—depending on which pied gene is combined.

The cinnamon gene reduces all the black colour to brown and the pied gene removes the psittacin and melanin pigments in patches—turning them yellow and white.

Fallow Pied

I cannot confirm if this combination has been produced—although there is no reason why not. The fallow gene would reduce the black plumage to brown and the pied gene would change the red plumage to yellow—a similar appearance to the Cinnamon Pied.

Combining the cinnamon gene would produce a Cinnamon Fallow Pied.

European Blue Recessive Pied—possibly a 'Black-eyed Clear' Blue combination

European Cinnamon Recessive Pied Crimson Rosella

European Blue Recessive Pied Crimson Rosella

INSET: Juvenile Blue Recessive Pied

European Cinnamon Blue Pied Crimson Rosella

European Cinnamon Blue Pied Crimson Rosella

European Cinnamon Seagreen Recessive Pied Crimson Rosella

European Dilute Pied Crimson Rosella

European Seagreen Dominant Pied Crimson Rosella

Dark Factor

The presence of a genuine 'dark factor' gene has not been confirmed. I have included the following probable colours as a matter of record.

Dark Factor Blue

Although I have been unable to find any reference to a Dark Factor Blue Crimson Rosella, a stunning 'Dark Factor Blue Pied' has been reported in Austria and the Czech Republic. Another mutation named 'Dark Factor Dilute Blue' has been reported in Germany.

'Dark Factor' Pied

This combination is only present in Germany. It would require the combination of two dominant genes or a dominant and a recessive gene—depending on which pied gene is used.

'Cinnamon Dark Factor'

This is another combination that I can only find reference to in Germany. It produces a bird displaying a greater intensity in yellow colouration. However, I am unsure where the 'dark' gene originated. The result may be a slight colour variation and not a genuine 'Dark Factor' mutation. Considerable research is needed to confirm this.

Combined with the blue gene it will produce 'Cinnamon Dark Blue' or 'Cinnamon Double Dark Blue'.

'Dilute Yellow Dark Factor'

Hans Biscoping of Germany has identified what he referred to as a 'Yellow Dilute Olive'. It was not possible to confirm the exact genetic makeup prior to publication.

A possible 'Cinnamon Dark Factor' Crimson Rosella hen bred in Europe

A possible 'Dark Factor Blue Pied' Crimson Rosella juvenile hen bred in Europe

A possible 'Dilute Yellow Dark Factor' Crimson Rosella bred in Europe

P ODEKERKEN

Yellow Rosella

YELLOW ROSELLA
Platycercus flaveolus

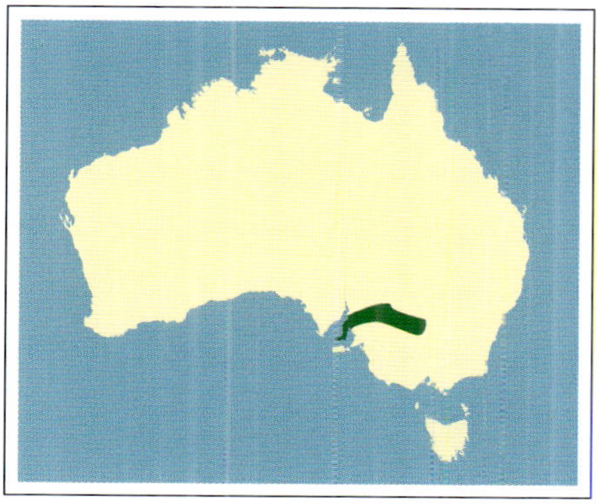

Other Names
Murrumbidgee Rosella, Murray Smoker, River Rosella, Yellow-rumped Rosella
German: Strohsittich
Dutch: Strogele Rosella
French: Perruche à couleur paille

DESCRIPTION

Adult
Length: 35cm
Average weight: 130 grams
Iris: Brown
Legs: Grey
Beak: Horn

There are many parrot species mistakenly identified as Yellow Rosellas. The superficially similar Green Rosella and the paler Adelaide Rosella are both regularly mistaken as Yellow Rosellas. Some consider the Yellow Rosella to be a subspecies of the Crimson Rosella.

Cock
The head, chest and abdomen are bright yellow, sometimes edged with orange-red and the frontal band is orange-red. The cheekpatches are violet blue and the mantle and wing-coverts are black, edged with yellow. The shoulder-patches are blue and the central tail feathers are blue and tinged with olive-green. The outer tail feathers are blue merging to pale blue and tipped with white.

Yellow Rosella cock

Yellow Rosella hen

Hen

Colouration is similar to the cock. The hen displays slight sexual dimorphism, generally showing more orange-red through the chest and throat area. The hen is usually shorter and smaller in size than the cock.

Juvenile

Juveniles display a smaller and paler red frontal brow than the adult. There is variation seen in some fledglings which display a duller version of the adult plumage. The overall plumage colour is dull yellow and the lower body area is a dull olive-green colour. Wing-coverts are dull olive-yellow and there is little scalloping on the mantle and back area, giving the overall appearance of a dull olive-green. The underwing stripe is visible.

Yellow Rosella hen (left) and juvenile cock

Subspecies and Racial Variations

The Yellow Rosella was first described as *Platycercus flaveolus* by John Gould in 1837, although this was challenged by Gregory Mathews, who claimed John Latham first described the Yellow Rosella as a 'Sulphur-headed Parrot' in 1822.

There are no subspecies of the Yellow Rosella.

IN THE WILD

The range of the Yellow Rosella extends from the Murrumbidgee and Murray River systems of New South Wales and Victoria to the lower reaches of the Lachlan and Darling River systems of south-

Wild Yellow Rosella pair in Hattah-Kulkyne National Park

western New South Wales, where the species can be found in large Red River Gums *Eucalyptus camaldulensis*. Seldom are these birds found far from such watercourses and their associated flood plains, although they can be found as far south as Mannum in South Australia and as far north as Tilpa and Menindee in western New South Wales.

Their habitat includes parklands and gardens in towns, as well as farms and orchards. This species is classed as common throughout its restricted range, but is threatened by irrigation schemes removing riverside forest in some areas.

Yellow Rosellas feed on Red River Gums, grass seeds, native berries, fruits and seeds as well as the introduced Scotch Thistle *Onopordon acanthium*. They have been recorded to consume the seeds of paddy melons *Cucumis myriocarpus*. Although they will consume cultivated fruits, they do not cause as much orchard damage as some other rosella species.

Breeding generally occurs from August to January. Nests are located in hollow limbs or holes in the trunk of living or dead trees, sometimes in the water. Between four and five eggs are incubated by the hen for approximately 19 days. Chicks fledge approximately 35 days after hatching.

IN CAPTIVITY

Status

The Yellow Rosella is uncommon in Australian aviculture, which I suspect is due to a lack of available mutations in this species. They are reasonably common in European aviaries but rare in the USA and New Zealand.

While generally considered to be not as aggressive as some of the other rosella species, Trevor Davis—a well-known South Australian breeder—regards the Yellow Rosella to be the *most* aggressive of the entire rosella genus. He has kept many pairs over the years and, in his experience, cocks often turn on the hens—even after several years of successful breeding.

Housing

Being one of the larger rosella species, the Yellow Rosella requires an aviary of similar size to the Crimson Rosella, measuring approximately 3.5–5 metres long x 1.2 metres wide x 2.4 metres high. One metre wide aviaries are adequate, however extra width will accommodate the larger nesting boxes or logs required by this species. Extra width also allows for easier cleaning of the aviary, particularly when the nests are in place.

All rosella species should be limited to one pair per aviary as dominant birds may become aggressive during the breeding season.

Breeding

The Yellow Rosella will accept logs or nestboxes for breeding. Nestboxes similar to those used for Crimson and Adelaide Rosellas, measuring approximately 600–900mm deep x 240mm square, with an inspection door in the side and a natural hollow or man-made spout fitted to the entrance, are ideal. I prefer removable lids on my nestboxes so they may be taken off in extreme hot temperatures.

Yellow Rosellas will breed in their first year and good pairs will double brood. Breeding usually occurs in August or September. Up to eight eggs can be laid, but between four and five is more usual. Incubation commences with the laying of the second or third egg and lasts for approximately 20 days. Fledging usually occurs approximately 30 to 35 days after hatching. Young should be removed from the parents after approximately two weeks or at the first sign of aggression from the cock.

Australian Cinnamon Yellow Rosella juvenile hen at various stages of development

PRIMARY COLOUR MUTATIONS

Cinnamon

A Cinnamon mutation is currently under development by a very experienced aviculturist in New South Wales.

This mutation is believed to be of sex-linked inheritance and displays all the black areas reduced to brown or pale fawn and the blue areas diluted to powder blue. The feet are flesh-coloured and the eyes are plum. The beak is horn-coloured.

The Cinnamon Yellow Rosella is available in Europe—further information was unavailable at the time of publication.

'Dilute'

The 'Dilute' mutation was under development by an aviculturist in South Australia, however the bird died during the writing of this book. Little was understood about the mutation, except that it produced a black-eyed bird with normal-coloured grey feet. The flight feathers were off-white and the scalloping on the mantle was grey rather than black. This bird was a cock, which suggests a recessive mutation. The successful establishment of this mutation will be extremely difficult, despite the production of a number of splits.

In the original edition of *A Guide to Rosellas* (1990) there was a photograph (pictured here) of a yellow bird, which appeared to be a possible 'Dilute' mutation. The flights and scalloping on the mantle were fawn and the blue areas were diluted to powder blue. This bird was believed to have been of recessive inheritance but I have been unable to find any more information about it. I doubt that it was ever established.

Australian 'Yellow' or 'Dilute' mutation of the Yellow Rosella—now extinct

Lutino

Still in the early stages of development, the Lutino mutation is understood to be sex-linked in its mode of inheritance. It produces a bird with red eyes, flesh-coloured feet and a red frontal band. All melanin is removed, leaving a yellow bird with white flights.

This mutation first appeared in Belgium in approximately 2003. Wayne Dempsey of New South Wales kept a Lutino Yellow Rosella many years ago but it never reproduced—this was the only reference of this mutation in Australia I had at the time of publication.

Pied ('Black-eyed Clear')

A white flighted Pied mutation is currently being developed in Victoria. This was initially considered to be a dominant mutation, however, I now believe it to be recessive in inheritance. I suspect the same pied-type 'Black-eyed Clear' mutation—as seen in the Australian Eastern Rosella and in the European Yellow, Crimson and Green Rosellas—will be developed. While progress has been slow, other white flighted birds have been produced and there is no reason why this mutation should not become established.

In Europe, a pied-type bird that appears to be another 'Black-eyed Clear' mutation has been established for a number of years.

European Lutino Yellow Rosella

This Australian Yellow Rosella juvenile displays pied markings. It is a possible visual split 'Black-eyed Clear' mutation

Australian Pied Yellow Rosella

Australian Pied Yellow Rosella

This European recessive 'Pied' Yellow Rosella is a typical example of a 'Black-eyed Clear' mutation

European 'Pied' Yellow Rosella—possibly a 'Dominant Edged' mutation

European pied-type Yellow Rosella of unknown inheritance

This is a recessive mutation—all red psittacin has been removed except for on the brow. The cheekpatches are white and there is a faint hint of blue on the shoulders. The flights are white and there are varying degrees of olive-green in patches on the mantle.

'Dominant Edged'

In Europe and New Zealand there appears to be a pied-type mutation, which could possibly be a 'Dominant Edged'. Further information was unavailable at the time of publication—however the New Zealand specimen, in particular, appears similar to the 'Dominant Edged' in other species.

This New Zealand bred Yellow Rosella appears to be a 'Dominant Edged' mutation

COMBINATIONS OF MUTATIONS

Cinnamon Pied

The only known combination of the Yellow Rosella that I am aware of is a Cinnamon Pied. This bird is only established in Europe, but could be produced in Australia in coming years. It is a combination of the sex-linked Cinnamon and the recessive Pied mutations.

European Cinnamon Pied Yellow Rosella

P ODEKERKEN

Adelaide Rosella cock

ADELAIDE ROSELLA
Platycercus adelaidae

Other Names
Adelaide Parrot, Pheasant Parakeet
German: Adelaidesittich
Dutch: Adelaide Rosella
French: Perruche Adelaide

DESCRIPTION

Adult
Length: 36cm
Weight: 150 grams
Iris: Brown
Legs: Grey
Beak: Grey-horn

No other species of rosella varies in colour as dramatically as the Adelaide Rosella—depending on the individual bird and geographic population.

The Adelaide Rosella is closely related to the Crimson and Yellow Rosella—and may even be a subspecies or racial variant. However, since this species is recognised by most aviculturists as separate, I have maintained that opinion for the purposes of this book.

Cock
The head, chest and abdomen plumage varies from orange or orange-yellow through to brick-red. The cheekpatches are violet-blue. The feathers of the mantle are black, edged with orange-yellow to orange-red, depending on the individual. Scapulars are black, shoulder-patches are blue and the flights are dark blue to black. The central tail feathers are dark blue merging to dark green on the edges. The outer tail feathers are dark blue diluting to pale blue and tipped with white. The rump and uppertail coverts are olive-yellow to orange-yellow.

Hen
Colouration is similar to the cock, although the hen may display similar variation in the plumage colouration, ranging from dull orange-yellow to orange-red.

The hen is usually slightly smaller in size—particularly the head and the mandible, which are smaller and finer than those of the cock.

Juvenile
Juveniles are a duller version of the adult. The head, neck and chest are a dull orange-yellow to orange-red and the lower chest and abdomen are a dull grey-green. Wings are dull olive, the rump is olive-yellow, the central tail feathers are dark olive and the underside of the tail is pale blue-grey. The underwing stripe is visible.

Adelaide Rosella hen

Subspecies and Racial Variations

The Adelaide Rosella was first described as *Platycercus adelaidae* by John Gould in 1840. The subspecies *Platycercus adelaidae subadelaidae* was first described by Gregory Mathews in 1912.

The former subspecies *P. a. fleurieuensis* was first described by E Ashby in 1917 as *Platycercus elegans fleurieuensis*. It is unclear how it became *Platycercus adelaidae fleurieuensis*—now considered a racial variation rather than a subspecies.

Adelaide Rosella P. a. subadelaidae cock (left) and hen. These two birds display the variation in chest colouration seen between individuals

P. a. subadelaidae

This subspecies is found in the northern parts of the southern Flinders Range and around Gawler and the Barossa Valley in South Australia.

These birds are more yellow with only marginal orange-red markings. At the northern part of the range, specimens are mostly yellow with minimal amounts of the orange seen in the nominate subspecies *P. a. adelaidae*.

Adelaide Rosella P. a. fleurieuensis hen

P. a. fleurieuensis

This racial variant is commonly named the 'Red Adelaide' by Australian aviculturists and is found around the Fleurieu Peninsula south of Adelaide and in the Deep Creek Conservation Park, South Australia.

These birds are a darker crimson-red compared to the orange-red colouration in the nominate subspecies.

IN THE WILD

The range of the Adelaide Rosella centres around the Fleurieu Peninsula, north to the Mount Lofty Ranges and the southern Flinders Range, east towards the Murray River and west towards Port Augusta in South Australia.

Their habitat includes parks and gardens around the outskirts of Adelaide, open forest, timbered valleys, farmlands and orchards. In the drier Flinders Range area they are generally found near watercourses. They are reasonably common throughout the range and are observed in pairs and small groups.

Wild Adelaide Rosella P. a. fleurieuensis photographed at Victor Harbour, South Australia

Adelaide Rosellas feed on eucalypt, mallee, acacia and grevillea trees and shrubs as well as on seeding grasses, weeds, flowers, nectar, shrubs, nuts, fruits, berries and insects and their larvae. They are considered pests by orchard growers in the Adelaide Hills region.

Breeding generally occurs from August to January. Nests are located at a 30–40 degree angle high up in the hollows of living or dead eucalypts, often close to water. The nesting chamber is located close to the entrance. Four to five eggs are incubated by the hen for approximately 19 days. Chicks fledge approximately 35 days after hatching.

IN CAPTIVITY

Status

The Adelaide Rosella is not held in large numbers in Australian aviaries, particularly outside South Australia. They are reasonably common throughout Europe.

They have a reputation as being hard to breed. I suspect that poor pair compatibility has contributed largely to this situation, with most aviculturists pairing odd birds hoping they will be compatible, rather than introducing birds when they are young and allowing them to select their own mates.

Of the several pairs I have owned, only one pair has ever bred and this was the subspecies *P. a. fleuriensis*.

Housing

The Adelaide Rosella requires an aviary of similar size to the Crimson Rosella—measuring approximately 4–5 metres long x 1.2 metres wide x 2.1 metres high.

They should be limited to one pair per aviary as dominant cocks may become aggressive during the breeding season and injure or kill the hens.

Breeding

The Adelaide Rosella will accept logs or nestboxes for breeding. Nestboxes measuring 600–900mm long x 230mm square with a natural hollow spout or a man-made spout fixed to the front, are ideal. The entrance hole should measure approximately 90mm in diameter. This species will nest in boxes without lids.

Generally, Adelaide Rosellas do not breed until at least two years of age. They will double brood, but this is not common. Breeding usually occurs from September to December. Up to eight eggs can be laid, although it is rare for more than five or six to actually hatch. Incubation commences with the laying of the third or fourth egg and lasts for approximately 19 days. Fledging occurs approximately 35 days after hatching, or earlier during high temperatures.

PRIMARY COLOUR MUTATIONS

Blue

I believe that a Blue mutation was acquired by Gerry Rutte of South Australia in the late 1990s. This bird has reproduced, however there was little information available at the time of publication. The mode of inheritance is recessive.

At the time of publication I had not found any information on any Blue mutation bred in Europe.

Australian Blue Adelaide Rosella cock

Cinnamon

The mode of inheritance for the Cinnamon mutation is always sex-linked.

I believe that Stan Sindel was the first to breed the Cinnamon mutation in Australia from stock originating from a wild-caught hen during the mid–1980s.

The current Cinnamon mutation birds were established by Gerry Rutte from birds legally taken from the wild in 1989.

This mutation is rare in Australia as many younger birds have failed to reproduce—possibly due to incompatible pairs.

In this attractive mutation the blue plumage on the cheek, shoulders and tail feathers is diluted to a powder blue colour and the black areas on the mantle and flights are reduced to a light brown or biscuit colour. Chicks hatch with plum-coloured eyes that darken with age. The feet and toenails are flesh-coloured.

The Cinnamon mutation is not common in Europe. It appears to be the same or very similar to the Australian Cinnamon mutation.

Australian Cinnamon Adelaide Rosella cock

European Cinnamon Adelaide Rosella

Australian NSL Lutino Adelaide Rosella cock

Australian sex-linked Lutino Adelaide Rosella

Lutino

There are two modes of inheritance for the Lutino mutation—sex-linked and recessive, also identified as non sex-linked (NSL). Very little is understood about the sex-linked mutation in the Adelaide Rosella and I would classify it as extremely rare in Australia.

The impressive NSL Lutino mutation displays red eyes. The body plumage is yellow with a red tint on some feathers. The cheekpatches, flights and tail are white. The lutino gene does not alter red, therefore the red brow remains.

Despite the rarity of the sex-linked Lutino mutation in this species, Gerry Rutte kept a Lutino hen in the late 1990s, however it did not survive.

The NSL mutation is also rare in Australia and is only kept by a couple of breeders. Col Gunter of Tamworth, New South Wales, kept a NSL Lutino cock in his collection for a number of years. Fortunately, a number of split birds were produced before the cock died. Much work must be done to establish this mutation.

At the time of publication I had been unable to find any information regarding this mutation in Europe.

Australian Pied Adelaide Rosella—the live version of the mounted specimen on the right

Pied

A few birds displaying white flights exist in Australian aviaries, however little is understood of their mode of inheritance. I suspect they are recessive and once established will produce full Pied or 'Black-eyed Clear' birds as seen in the Eastern, Crimson, Yellow and Green Rosellas.

For many years Col Gunter had in his collection a pied-type bird that displayed pied markings over most of the plumage. Unfortunately this bird never reproduced—it was quite old at the time of death.

COMBINATIONS OF MUTATIONS

None known.

Australian Pied Adelaide Rosella

Green Rosella

GREEN ROSELLA
Platycercus caledonicus

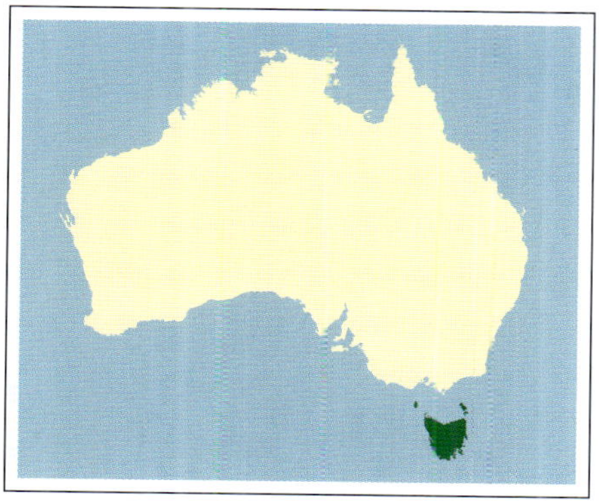

Other Names
Tasmanian Rosella, Yellow-bellied Rosella, Mountain Parrot
German: Gelbbauchsittich
Dutch: Geelbuik Rosella
French: Perruche à ventre jaune

DESCRIPTION

Adult
Length: 37cm
Weight: 170 grams
Iris: Brown
Legs: Grey
Beak: Horn

Due to the geographic isolation of the Green Rosella, this species has evolved into a very distinctive member of the genus. It is the largest of the rosellas and has an extensive range in a number of habitats throughout Tasmania and the Bass Strait islands.

Cock
The plumage of the head, chest and abdomen is a rich yellow colour and the head displays a wide red frontal band. The cheekpatches are deep blue and the mantle is black, edged with dark green. The shoulder-patches are violet blue and the flights are blue merging to black at the tips. The undertail coverts are washed with orange-red and the uppertail coverts are bright olive. The central tail feathers are dull bronze and tipped with blue and the outer tail feathers are blue diluting to pale blue on the edges. The rump is olive. Some specimens display an orange-red wash to the vent and chest.

Hen
Colouration is similar to the cock, although the overall plumage is generally duller. The mandible is smaller and narrower. The throat and upper chest are usually washed with orange-red.

Green Rosella cock

Green Rosella hen

Green Rosella juvenile cock

Juvenile

Juveniles generally display more yellow-green on the head, nape and body than the adult.

They also lack the distinctive black scalloping seen in mature birds. The undertail coverts are dull green with yellow-green edges and the abdomen is yellow. The tail feathers are dark blue with pale tips. The underwing stripe is visible.

Subspecies and Racial Variations

The Green Rosella was first described as *Psittacus caledonicus* by Johann Gmelin in 1788. However, in 1781 John Latham described it as the 'Caledonian Parrot' from a specimen collected at Adventure Bay, Tasmania. This specimen was originally believed to have originated from New Caledonia, hence the name *Psittacus caledonicus*.

When the mistake was uncovered, several other names were suggested—*Psittacus brownii* by Kuhl in 1820, *Psittacus flavigaster* by Temminck in 1821 and *Psittacus flaviventri* by Temminck at a later date.

The present name *Platycercus caledonicus* was given by Wagler in 1832.

Gregory Mathews proposed the name *Platycercus caledonicus henriettoe* for the King Island subspecies in 1915 and *Platycercus caledonicus flindersi* for the Flinders Island subspecies in 1917. However, neither are presently recognised subspecies and are classified as racial variations.

P. c. flindersi

This variation from Flinders Island is small and dark in overall colouration, with a green vent.

P. c. henriettoe

This variation from King Island is larger with more red on the head and vent area than the nominate subspecies.

IN THE WILD

The range of the Green Rosella extends across Tasmania to the offshore islands of Bass Strait. Their habitat includes orchards, farmlands, eucalypt forest, rainforest and woodlands all over Tasmania—except in areas lacking timber. Some birds can also be found in urban parks and gardens. They are common throughout the range, but appear to be declining on King Island due to land clearing.

They are generally observed in pairs or family groups and their loud calls are often heard in forested areas. They are regularly seen feeding on spilled grain on farmlands—frequently in the company of Eastern Rosellas *P. e. diemenensis* also residing in the wild in Tasmania.

Green Rosellas feed on a wide range of seeding grasses, berries, fruits, the flowers of shrubs and eucalypts and insects and their larvae. They can cause extensive crop damage, particularly to hawthorn hedges.

Breeding generally occurs from November to February. Nests are usually located in the hollows of dead or living eucalypts. Some nests have also been found in former convict buildings at Port Arthur. Between four and six eggs are incubated by the hen for approximately 19 days. Chicks fledge approximately 35 days after hatching.

The Green Rosella is a beautiful species that is unfortunately held in low numbers in captivity

IN CAPTIVITY

Status

The Green Rosella is quite rare in Australian aviculture. Although held in reasonable numbers in Europe, it is almost extinct in the USA and New Zealand.

Housing

The Green Rosella requires a cool environment to breed successfully during warm temperatures. Being cold climate birds, they usually moult during warm weather, which halts any attempt to breed. Some Crimson Rosellas are known to act in a similar way. Aviaries covered with shadecloth or located under large trees are essential in warmer climates.

Cocks tend to suffer with obesity, therefore aviaries should measure a minimum of 5 metres long x 1.2 metres wide x 2.1 metres high. Breeding pairs should be housed as one pair per aviary to reduce aggression and fighting.

Although I have never kept this species, I have found it effective with other rosella species to wrap nestboxes with wet hessian bags on very hot days to lower the internal temperature. Care must be taken to remove the bags before nightfall in case the chicks become too cold. Other aviculturists place air conditioners in aviaries housing Green Rosellas to keep the environment cool and encourage breeding.

The Green Rosella requires a cool environment to successfully rear young

Breeding

Green Rosella chicks bred in Australia

The Green Rosella will accept logs or nestboxes for breeding. Open top logs measuring a minimum of 1500mm deep with an internal diameter of 250mm and with the base sitting on the floor of the aviary are ideal, particularly in hot areas. Nestboxes measuring 900mm long x 250mm square are also acceptable. An entrance hole measuring a minimum of 100mm in diameter is required.

Green Rosellas will breed at two to three years of age. It is possible for the birds to double brood, but this is not common. Breeding usually occurs from October to December. Between three and six eggs are laid. Incubation commences with the laying of the second or third egg and lasts for approximately 20 days. Fledging occurs approximately 35 days after hatching.

Trevor Davis of South Australia had success breeding Green Rosellas on Kangaroo Island off the South Australian coast. These birds consistently laid five or six eggs and reared four to five chicks, often double brooding. They stopped breeding when Trevor moved to Murray Bridge, inland South Australia, where the temperatures were much higher.

Interesting observations noted by both Trevor and Paul Stubbington indicated that Green Rosellas have a strong odour—similar to a musty smell. The reason is unknown as the observed birds were all in excellent condition and achieved terrific breeding results.

PRIMARY COLOUR MUTATIONS

Cinnamon or Dilute

There is a photograph of a mounted specimen of a possible 'Cinnamon' or 'Dilute' mutation published in Stan Sindel and James Gill's book *Australian Broad-tailed Parrots—the Platycercus and Barnardius Geneva* (1999).

Pied

Pied and Normal Green Rosella chicks bred in Europe

German breeder Uwe Hanisch has been developing a Pied mutation in the Green Rosella for a number of years.

The mode of inheritance is reported to be dominant, however after viewing photographs, it appears that this mutation may be recessive and therefore classified as a 'Black-eyed Clear' mutation.

This bird displays full pied markings with some green on the mantle feathers. The

Pied Green Rosella cock

Pied Green Rosella juvenile

blue cheekpatches and the red brow are retained. There is a slight blue tinge on the shoulder-patches and the flights are white. The feet are flesh-coloured and the toenails are clear. Some specimens display varying degrees of blue on the tail feathers.

These birds were bred from parents displaying small amounts of pied markings and white flights. They may be split Pied birds that display breakthrough pied markings as is seen in the Black-eyed Clear mutation. They are similar in appearance to the Australian Pied Eastern Rosella and the European Pied Yellow Rosella.

I believe that if more Green Rosellas were kept and bred in captivity, then many of the mutations that exist in other rosella species could be developed in this species.

This Green Rosella exhibits greater red colouration through the head and chest

Colour Variations

Green Rosellas displaying varying degrees of red colouration through the chest have been reported in various literature since the 1950s. Marcus Pollard of Tasmania has bred birds exhibiting a variation in the degree of red colouration on the head and chest.

COMBINATIONS OF MUTATIONS

None known.

BIBLIOGRAPHY

ABK Publications 1990, *A Guide to Australian Long and Broad-tailed Parrots and New Zealand Kakarikis—their Management, Care and Breeding*, ABK Publications, New South Wales, Australia, *www.birdkeeper.com.au*.

ABK Publications 1990, *A Guide to Rosellas and their Mutations*, ABK Publications, New South Wales, Australia.

Birds Australia 2009, *Conservation through knowledge—Birds Australia*, *http://www.birdsaustralia.com.au*.

California Vegetable Specialties 2008, *Endive world—Home of California vegetable specialties*, *http://www.endive.com*.

Foodconsumer.org 2009, *http://www.fooddatabase.com*.

Forshaw, JM 1980, *Australian Parrots*, Landsdowne Press, Melbourne, Victoria, Australia.

Hagen Avicultural Research Institute, 2007, *Home page*, *http://www.hagen.com/hari*.

Harman, I 1981, *Australian Parrots—in Bush and Aviary*, Inkata Press, Melbourne, Victoria, Australia.

Lendon, AH 1989, *Australian Parrots in Field and Aviary*, 2nd edn, Angus & Robertson, Australia.

Parrot Society of Australia Incorporated, 2008, *http://www.parrotsociety.org.au*.

Shephard, M 1994, *Aviculture in Australia—Keeping and Breeding Aviary Birds*, 2nd edn, Reed Books, Chatswood, New South Wales, Australia.

Sindel S & Gill, J 1999, *Australian Broad-tailed Parrots—the Platycercus and Barnardius Genera*, Singil Press, New South Wales, Australia.

The George Mateljan Foundation, 2009, *The world's healthiest foods*, *http://www.whfoods.com*.

Yahoo 2009, *Genetics: Psittacine*, *http://pets.groups.yahoo.com/group/Genetics-Psittacine/*.

Zomer HPM 2006, *Rosella's en hun kleurmutaties (Rosellas and their colour mutations)*, Uitgeverij Herman Zomer, Giethoorn, The Netherlands.

Words on Birds...

ABK Publications
PO Box 6288, Tweed Heads South NSW 2486 AUSTRALIA
Telephone: +61 7 5590 7777 • Facsimile: +61 7 5590 7130
email: birdkeeper@birdkeeper.com.au • website: www.birdkeeper.com.au